Portraits
of Collaboration

edited by
Andrea Honigsfeld
Maria G. Dove

Published by Seidlitz Education
P.O. Box 166827
Irving, TX 75016
www.seidlitzeducation.com

For related titles and support materials visit www.seidlitzeducation.com.

8.22

Contents

Preface

Andrea Honigsfeld and
Maria G. Dove

In her book *The Gifts of Imperfection,* Brené Brown (2010)[1] defines connection as "the energy that exists between people when they feel seen, heard, and valued; when they can give and receive without judgment; and when they derive sustenance and strength from the relationship" (p. 19). In our many years of experience with investigating collaborative practices among educators, and from our own personal experiences collaborating with one another as well as other professionals, making authentic connections as Brown describes is fundamental to effective teamwork. It is no wonder that when teachers genuinely share their personal experiences with the craft of teaching, their collaborations are ultimately more meaningful in strengthening, extending, revising, and inspiring their teaching practices. Much of this is due to teachers feeling that they are being seen, heard, and valued in their partnerships.

In this volume, we wanted to share with our readers the unadulterated, straight-from-the-shoulder collaborative experiences of teachers currently working in the field for the sake of multilingual learners (MLs). In doing so, this unique set of practitioners can share how they work in tandem to support an integrated service delivery for MLs, incorporating the collaborative instructional cycle—co-planning, co-teaching, co-assessment, and reflection—as a framework for their teamwork. Our authors highlight various aspects of the collaborative instructional cycle such as how to prepare lessons for language and content integration, develop co-planning routines, co-deliver instruction, and create processes for co-assessment. Moreover, they offer a fresh take on noteworthy practices such as peer coaching and consultation, relationship building, innovative use of technology, and collaboration with multiple teams. In many ways, our authors chronicle how teacher collaboration shapes the hearts and souls of their school communities.

We would like to stress that our aim for this project was to cultivate a sense of authenticity about the unique experiences of each of our contributing authors. In doing so, we strived to ensure the chapters in this volume are faithful accounts of the practices, insights, and actions behind each author's work in the field. Their individual experiences have informed their writing styles to best capture

---

[1] Brown, B. (2010). *The gifts of imperfection: Let go of who you think you're supposed to be and embrace who you are*. Hazelden.

their journeys of collaboration. It is our hope that their personal portrayals will be a valuable resource to assist both novice and experienced teachers in enhancing their collaborative practices for the sake of MLs.

To pique your curiosity here is an overview of what you'll find in each chapter:

In Chapter 1, Allyson Caudill, John Cox, and Ashley Blackley—known as the ReadySetCoteach team—draw attention to the power of collaboration triads. In order to expand their collaboration initiative to ensure that their English learners (ELs) remained successful in subsequent school years, they began to collaborate not just within their grade levels as co-teaching teams but across grade levels as well, creating a collaboration triad consisting of a first-grade teacher, a second-grade teacher, and an English as a Second Language (ESL) teacher. They describe how this team arrangement ensured a level of consistency in their teaching routines, language supports, and high expectations over the course of multiple years for all students.

In Chapter 2, Brittany Schmidt and Carmen O'Brien recount their unique opportunity for collaboration. They describe how a retractable wall situated between their classrooms allowed them to turn their two classes into one. They show how they took advantage of the setup to plan lessons for all students, configure their joint class for co-teaching, use strategies and tools for instruction, successfully accomplish assessment tasks, and reflect on their practices.

In Chapter 3, Lindsay Manzella and Jane Russell Valezy showcase their multifaceted experiences working with middle school teachers to support English language learners (ELLs) in a nonprofit international school. They detail how their program model shifted from what most would consider traditional methods of teaching ELLs to a model that supported content teachers' successful delivery of content and language instruction through consultation, collaboration, and coaching.

In Chapter 4, Jackie Griffin and Stephanie Just detail their co-assessment practices using formative and summative assessments. They highlight the importance of knowing and understanding learning benchmarks in order to create appropriate assessments, discussing with team members when assessments are needed, and spending time analyzing data with their co-teaching partners to plan future instruction. They emphasize providing a variety of assessments for students to demonstrate their learning, focusing on lessons that provide practice in the four language domains to assess language development, and using backward planning to ensure both content and language are being addressed.

In Chapter 5, Katie Toppel spotlights how kindergarten and first-grade classes in her school made a shift to co-teaching and teacher collaboration to better align content and language instruction for English learners. She discusses how she best managed her time when she had to collaborate with multiple teams. She emphasizes the importance of long-term lesson planning, regular co-planning time, content alignment across classes on the same grade level, use of digital tools to share resources and materials, and high impact strategies to maximize co-planning effectiveness.

In Chapter 6, Michelle Gill focuses on how select schools in her district adopted the use of technology to plan and administer lessons to meet students' learning needs. She addresses how teacher teams worked together to map and align curricula and build lessons using a content and language lens. She shares the successes of school teams with supportive evidence from the norms of collaboration they developed, the planning guides that they used, the roadblocks they encountered, and the ways teacher teams problem-solved.

In Chapter 7, Sarah Bouwer and Tan Huynh examine the social-emotional components of relationship building by sharing how they developed a trusting, collaborative relationship. They discuss how they maintained an equal partnership, committed to using nonjudgmental language, established common understandings, and helped each other with tasks both big and small. They outline their lesson planning and instructional delivery, highlighting their many roles and responsibilities in the co-teaching relationship.

In Chapter 8, Valentina Gonzalez offers an in-depth look at the reluctant teacher, one who remains resistant to forming and participating in collaborative partnerships. She offers several unique ideas for getting teachers involved with collaborative practices and provides a blueprint for initiating and cultivating teacher collaboration. She suggests ways to plan for success, such as learning to talk less and listen more, aiming for parity, and promoting inclusion for English learners.

While the idea for this volume was born several years ago, the final chapter is a newer addition to the stories that come before it. The previous eight chapters share powerful examples of collaboration, representing practices that originated before COVID-19 shuttered schools around the United States and globally. Before March of 2020, the contributing authors and the editorial team members had collaborated about collaboration for many months. They were looking forward to the launch of this book, to celebrate the many different forms of collaboration for the sake of multilingual learners. It was originally scheduled to be released right around the height of the pandemic. Ironically, the crisis that disrupted our personal and professional lives both delayed the book's publication and brought about new opportunities for teachers to connect with each other, strengthen existing relationships, develop new partnerships, and explore innovative mediums for collaboration. In order to explore these unprecedented efforts by teachers to remain connected with one another during the pandemic, we invited Kristina Robertson to join the project as a collaborating author of the final chapter. Her enthusiasm for contributing to this work and her experience working with English learners/multilingual learners (ELs/MLs) is best captured by this comment:

> *In my 25 years in the EL/ML field, I have never seen such a dramatic transformation among all educators to collaborate with EL teachers, learn more about multilingual students, and reach out intentionally to multilingual families in multiple ways. The pandemic may actually be a "problemtunity" because from this chaos, educators developed skills and a vision for new ways of reaching and teaching EL/ML students and developing partnerships with their families. Let's not "return to normal"; rather, let's keep the good things and return to better.*

Together with Andrea and Maria, Kristina helped gather stories of continued collaboration from our 14 authors and synthesized those experiences in our final chapter. Together, they share a vision of a more collaborative future for addressing the education of our students. ● ● ●

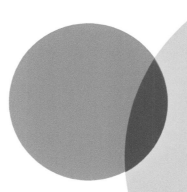

Foreword

In my thirties, I enrolled in an alternative certification program to become a special education teacher. With no experience, I began teaching multilingual learners within a year. Thankfully, my principal paired me up with Jeanne Bellosillo, a master special education teacher. I will always be grateful, because our collaborations allowed me to accomplish so much more than I could have imagined. I learned early on that, beyond Jeanne, there were many colleagues who could help me grow quickly if I was open to support. Teaching multilingual learners identified as both special education and ESL was so challenging as a new teacher, but I was delighted by our progress. Collaboration was key for my growth and the growth of my students. We could all do more together.

Fast-forward many years, and by 2015 I was on special assignment in our district bilingual/ESL department. I was becoming more and more confident in my craft. That year, however, the demographics in one of our feeder patterns changed suddenly and drastically. Within just a few weeks, we had dozens and dozens of refugee students enrolling who were identified as SLIFE (Students with Limited or Interrupted Formal Education). I was reassigned to the middle school to support as a newcomer teacher. Again, I was out of my comfort zone and worried that I would fail these learners who had finally gotten to a place where they could take advantage of education. Sure enough, we had a rocky start. Things that had worked for me in the past were falling flat. But we eventually found great success, with the students exceeding my expectations.

Do you want to know what turned things around? Collaboration, of course. I was leaning on specialists from across the district, but one of my most valuable colleagues in this endeavor was a student teacher named Katherine Dierschke. She would split the class with me at times, and we would plan together. In this scenario, I was the veteran teacher, and my role was to help grow Katherine as a new educator. But we developed such a positive relationship that she was comfortable questioning and challenging my ideas.

Her fresh eyes were so important as we reflected on what was working and how we might try to boost the literacy and language of our students. Without question, the students, Katherine, and I were making great strides because we were all able to do more together.

In these challenging times, collaborating with others is more important than ever. Whether you are the seasoned veteran, the new educator, the specialist, or the mainstream teacher, *Portraits of Collaboration* will inspire you. It is filled with best practices for collaborating on behalf of multilingual learners, but it goes beyond that. Andrea Honigsfeld and Maria Dove have brought together experienced practitioners from across the field to offer us chapters of unfiltered, real-world experiences. The authors suggest ideas to overcome obstacles, they challenge our thinking, and they remind us to celebrate what we are accomplishing when we work with one another. What I wish for all educators is that they capitalize on the power of collaboration to bring everyone's talents together. As we see in each of these chapters, when we work collaboratively, we are not only growing, but we are also working smarter. And this is so important because, thankfully, we can all do more together.

Carol Salva
Dr. Carol Salva is an author and consultant with Seidlitz Education. She is a former newcomer teacher, bilingual teacher, and ESL specialist.

The Six
Elements
OF SUCCESSFUL CONTENT-LANGUAGE INTEGRATION

Allyson Caudill, John Cox, & Ashley Blackley

📷 SNAPSHOT

Our school is a Title 1 school with 714 total students in grades Pre-K through 5. Our community is urban, and we are located in North Carolina's largest school district, which comprises approximately 205 schools. We are ethnically diverse, and 80 percent of the school population is identified as economically disadvantaged. Our students speak 24 different languages, and roughly 200 are English learners (ELs), about 28 percent of the student body. Classes in grades K through 2 are self-contained, meaning teachers teach all subject areas. We have two ESL teachers assigned to our building; one serves grades K through 2, and the other serves 3 through 5. Four years ago, in the lower grades, we switched from a pull-out model to a collaborative model where ELs are clustered into certain classrooms and the ESL and content teacher co-teach during literacy.

SETTING THE STAGE

Our unique dynamic of Allyson, the ESL teacher, co-teaching with both Ashley (first grade) and John (second grade) has created a triad of collaboration, and if we're being honest, the collaboration was accidental. In early math instruction, students are taught about number relationships using the phrase "part, part, whole." We often apply these terms to explain our collaboration. As co-teachers, we are each one "part" of a co-teaching partnership, and each school year, students respond well to having two teachers co-plan, co-teach, co-assess, and co-reflect as a team. Yet, that is just one year of their school career. We asked ourselves how we could expand our collaboration initiative to ensure that our students remained successful in subsequent school years. In response, we started intentionally collaborating vertically as well—not just as two separate co-teaching pairs but across grade levels, too, as a triad. The three of us, as the "whole," can collaborate and ensure a level of consistency with our routines, language supports, and high expectations over the course of multiple years. Furthermore, when focusing on the "whole," we can collaborate with a shared vision, and our teaching has never been stronger.

Figure 1. Collaborative Practice
Created by Allyson Caudill, John Cox, and Ashley Blackley. Used with permission.

We used to teach content and language separately—Allyson in her ESL room and John and Ashley in their respective grade-level classrooms. Every day, Allyson would come pick up her handful of students and teach them verb tenses and vocabulary wholly disconnected from anything happening in the content classroom. Did students experience growth? Some, but we knew there had to be a more effective model. Now, instead of taking students out of class, we meet the needs of our school's diverse student body (93 percent minority, 31 percent ELs) by integrating content and language. In this inclusive environment, students achieve more. So, for the past four years, we have operated as a co-teaching triad: Allyson (ESL), John (second grade), and Ashley (first grade). We consistently co-plan and co-teach the English language arts block. The expertise that we all bring to the table has coalesced into a learning environment that is positive, engaging, and ultimately a perfect recipe for success for our ELs and general education students alike.

BLUEPRINT

THE POWER OF MERGING EXPERTISE

Separately, we are good teachers; together, we are great teachers. We've found that combining our individual knowledge, skills, and ideas increases our effectiveness as well as student success. Matching complementary strengths enhances our collaboration and co-teaching because the content teachers (John and Ashley) are the experts on grade-level content while the ESL teacher (Allyson) is the language expert. Merging our expertise is powerful because we are able to develop rigorous content lessons within a language-rich environment, and we learn from each other in the process. There are six elements of collaboration we follow to maximize our collective knowledge and meet the needs of all students.

Share

Before we can even begin to collaborate, we need to know (and we mean really know) our shared students. Each year, we sit down and look at our class lists and Allyson's caseload together. We go over all of the background information and language proficiency data Allyson has on the identified ELs and we make

Teacher
Data
collection

Mrs. Blackley & Ms. Caudill

copies for all of us. We look at the WIDA (World-Class Instructional Design and Assessment) Can-Do Descriptors and discuss expectations. Then, we do the same with the native English-speaking students, with Ashley and John leading the way. This sharing of information is essential to achieving the highest level of effectiveness for our ELs because in order to meet their needs, we have to know what their needs are.

Quick Tips

- Make student data accessible to all collaborators.
- Use folders, an online shared drive, or a notebook.
- Create a plan to share new information frequently and in a timely manner.
- Avoid "handoffs" of information without collaborative discussion or an opportunity to unpack the information's value.

6 Elements of Effective Collaboration

1. Share information
What student information or data do I have? What data or information does my collaborator have to offer?

2. Create a Communication Plan
As collaborators, how and when will we communicate?

3. Integrate
What strengths do we each bring to the table? How can we combine expertise to increase our impact?

4. Cooperate & Collaborate
In what ways can we expand our collaborative practice to include other professionals?

5. Reflect Together
What results are we seeing? What are our glows and grows as collaborators?

6. Make Adjustments
Based on our reflections, what changes can we make to improve our partnership and student outcomes?

Figure 2. Six Elements of Effective Collaboration
Created by Allyson Caudill, John Cox, and Ashley Blackley. Used with permission.

Communicate

Clear and consistent communication between content teachers and language specialists can be the deciding factor in student success. Determine *how* and *when* you will communicate and share information throughout the year. The truth is, ELs spend 75 percent of their day in content classrooms. No matter the caliber of language instruction ELs receive in a scheduled ESL class, if these same language supports and strategies aren't being implemented for the rest of their day, student growth will be limited. Think of it like this:

> You have a bowl full of sick fish. You take a couple out and nurse them back to health. If you put them right back in the same bowl, they will become sick all over again. Unless the fishbowl itself is rehabilitated, the cycle continues. To create a healthy bowl, content teachers and language specialists must communicate and work together to create the best environment for ELs to access the content and thrive in their own classrooms.

One of the most common questions we get asked is, *How do you find the time?* Our not-so-secret answer is that we utilize the cloud. Before Allyson started co-teaching, she communicated with content teachers by creating a shared drive with memos describing the objectives, activities, and resources of each ESL class. The content teachers could see what their students were doing language-wise, leave notes and comments for the ESL teacher about possible content connections, and ask questions if needed. Likewise, in our first year of co-teaching, we set up a shared Google Drive we could all access. We keep everything from to-do lists to lesson plans to blog posts in our drive and can access and work on them anytime, from anywhere. If we're working on a collective project and one of us hops on the drive to work, we text the other two to let them know. Whoever is available can jump on and contribute from wherever they are, and there's even a chat box so we can "talk" things over in the process.

However, working through the cloud doesn't replace our face-to-face meetings. Sitting down in person at least once a week is vital to our success as collaborators. Our conversation and communication can flow openly without the pause of checking a phone or life interrupting our agenda. When we sit down for a face-to-face meeting, we know that we are giving our full and undivided attention to each other.

Quick Tips

- Open and maintain lines of communication.
- Create a mutually agreed-upon communication plan.
- Keep an open-door policy.
- Initiate crucial conversations.
- Always assume positive intent.

Integrate

Pre-plan Separately: We have found that to be successful and efficient collaborators, we need to be prepared to plan together. Both teachers showing up to each meeting having already read the curriculum, standards, and any other resources for the week eliminates the need to waste time looking at lessons for the first time. Also, creating and sharing an agenda before meeting increases our productivity because each individual has an opportunity to digest the information, content, or work that will be discussed. Both teachers preparing ahead of time leads to increased productivity and ownership from all parties. If it is unclear what exactly should be reviewed before a meeting, ask. Content teachers can always provide the upcoming lessons, topics, or curriculum, and ESL teachers can provide the language standards, needs, and goals of ELs.

Quick Tips
- Come prepared.
- Know the standards and what to read and/or prep in advance.

Plan Collaboratively: Each week, we sit down together to co-plan with a purpose: to find ways to facilitate language acquisition through the content and curriculum. The goal is to teach language within a rich, meaningful context so students can acquire, practice, and internalize the academic language needed to succeed daily in the classroom. By collaborating, we minimize missed instructional time and simultaneously develop students' content knowledge and language skills. We meet once a week to plan our co-taught lessons for the week. During this time, Allyson can also assist John and Ashley with scaffolding ideas for other subjects. We always ask ourselves, *What academic language functions and skills are needed for students to be successful and participate fully in the lesson? How can we scaffold UP so students can access the content yet still be appropriately challenged?*

Effective co-teaching requires co-planning, but effective co-planning does not necessarily require co-teaching. ESL teachers can serve as sounding boards and language coaches for content teachers who are unable to co-teach. Two collaborators planning together means double the knowledge, which equals more ideas and an increased ability to meet the needs of diverse students, even if there is only one teacher actually delivering the instruction.

Quick Tips
- Set a consistent time and protect it.
- At the end of each meeting, set the agenda for the next meeting.
- Establish agreed-upon collaborative planning norms.
- Use a template.
- Know what you do (and don't) bring to the table.

For an example of an ELA lesson co-planned by John and Allyson that includes annotated language supports to meet the needs of all students, see pp. 28-29.

Cooperate

When we first started teaching together, we (Ashley & John) co-planned only with each other and then co-taught what we planned in our classroom behind closed doors. Allyson might have come into grade-level professional learning communities (PLCs) for a minute to share ACCESS* details or gather information to update EL plans, but she was not a regular participant in those meetings. The truth is that specialists and content teachers, whether co-teaching or not, share responsibility for student success. So, as we progressed further in our collaborative partnership, we realized the potential benefits of having both grade-level and

ESL teachers in grade-level PLCs. Now, we encourage all specialists we meet to try to get involved in school PLCs, at least for the grade levels they serve. We know scheduling can be a nightmare, but taking every opportunity to collaborate with the classroom teachers our students spend 80 to 90 percent of their time with can have a major impact on student learning.

Quick Tips

- Adopt a collaborative mindset.
- Think "our" students, "our" responsibilities.
- Keep a collaboration schedule.
- Invite relevant professionals into meetings and encourage their participation regularly.

* "ACCESS for ELLs (ACCESS) is the collective name for WIDA's suite of summative English language proficiency assessments. ACCESS is taken annually by English language learners in Kindergarten through Grade 12 in WIDA Consortium member states" (WIDA, 2021).

Benefits of Specialists Participating in Grade-Level PLCs

Collective ownership of grade-level expectations and needs

Significant advances in adapting teaching to reach all students

Strengthened parity in the eyes of colleagues and other school personnel (if co-teaching)

All teachers are informed of grade-level updates and events

Specialists become not just visitors but valued members of the team

Specialists are able to support more content teachers

10 Questions for Collaborative Reflection

1. What are our accomplishments as collaborators?
2. What upcoming challenges do we face?
   How can we overcome them together?
3. According to the data, what is working? What isn't working?
4. How can we apply all our expertise to better serve our students?
5. Is there anything we can change about our approach to make our collaborative efforts more effective?
6. On a scale of 1 to 10, how well is our communication plan working?
7. How can we strengthen our collaborative relationship?
8. In what ways can we support each other as collaborators?
9. What have we learned from each other thus far? What would we like to learn?
10. What are our goals for future collaboration?

Reflect

"The greatest effects on student learning occur when teachers become learners of their own teaching" (Hattie, 2009, p. 22). The difference between mediocrity and excellence is continuous reflection. We co-reflect regularly, purposefully communicating and checking in along the way. We even added a space in our lesson plan template for jotting down reflections as a team each week—both the "glows" and the "grows." These reflections are our opportunity to celebrate successes together and collaboratively solve problems when needed. In addition to our weekly reflections, we meet and reflect more extensively at the end of each school year. Co-reflecting can be uncomfortable at first, but it's key to improving our practice. Collaborators who reflect together grow together.

Quick Tips

- Start a reflection journal.
- Reflect frequently—both formally and informally.
- Be open and honest, and trust the process.
- Remember feedback is for growth, not judgment.

Adjust

The purpose of reflection is to ensure we are making decisions that positively impact our students' progress and help us develop our expertise. However, reflection without action is not enough. Knowing this, the final step in our collaborative cycle is to make professional and instructional adjustments based upon our reflections. Considering questions like *What changes can we make to improve our collaborative partnership?* and *What revisions will improve student outcomes?* help us turn reflection into actionable next steps, and those next steps into results.

Quick Tips

- Record next steps.
- Put your plan in writing to help hold yourself accountable and make sure everyone leaves on the same page.

HIGH IMPACT STRATEGIES

We found that three strategies have significantly contributed to our successful partnership. Relationship building, collaborative goal setting, and SWIRLing (speaking, writing, reading and listening through meaningful interactions) are nonnegotiables for us. Relationships are at the forefront of all good teaching and learning. Building and maintaining strong relationships will make or break your collaborative partnership and your shared success in the classroom. Collaborative goal setting helps strengthen our professional relationship and allows us to continue developing our shared and individual practices. Lastly, SWIRLing in the content areas gives co-teaching a purpose and foundation. Integrating content and language is vital for our students' achievement and growth.

Relationship Building

There are two types of relationships critical to our practice: relationships with students and relationships among collaborators.

Relationships with students: Teachers who create positive relationships with students are more likely to have above-average effects on student achievement (Hattie, 2009). We were asked once to write down at least two personal, non-academic facts about each of our students. It was eye-opening because we realized it was harder than we thought it would be. At that moment, we made a pact to know every student and build not just a classroom community, but a family. It is only through mutual trust, love, and respect that collaborators can achieve complete parity in the eyes of their students. We are fortunate to be able to have two teachers in the room, and it's an asset for students to see a real working relationship, healthy disagreements, and the use of effective communication skills. Different students also connect with different types of teachers, in terms of both personality and style. Our differences end up being a strength in relationship building because we find that students can usually connect and build a solid relationship with at least one of us. The stronger the relationship between teachers and students, the more likely it is for students to take risks, and that's how they grow.

We also use micro-affirmations in the classroom: small shout-outs that accentuate the positive and provide opportunities for students to build each other up. For example, students consistently receive feedback and encouragement from their peers, who call each other by name and use simple chants like, "You got this!" and, "Let's go (name)!" These small gestures not only build respect and rapport among peers and create a fun, engaging learning environment, but they also provide built-in wait time and lower students' affective filters so that learners feel they are in a safe space. When students share their work or ideas, their peers show respect by sitting up straight, making eye contact, and nodding when spoken to directly. We like to reward students for treating each other with respect, showing compassion, and encouraging others. It's great to watch students begin to see others' success as their own and the class as a family unit.

Relationships among collaborators:

When it comes to our relationship as collaborators, just like any relationship, it takes time and effort to build and maintain trust and respect. As collaborative practitioners, we keep our relationship at the forefront of our responsibilities, and we've learned three important lessons. First, we learned to have hard conversations, even if it's uncomfortable. Disagreements will happen. They are a natural part of any human interaction. Address the issues rather than letting any negative feelings fester. To help with this and show respect for one another, we developed norms for our meetings that will ensure everyone's needs are met. Second, always assume positive intent and try to see your collaborator's perspective. Starting there will set the relationship up for success. The third and final lesson we learned is that it's important to celebrate together. We celebrate the birthdays of all members of our PLC and set aside time in meetings to share positive experiences—both personal and professional. Besides intentionally planning our PLCs to celebrate these positive experiences, we purposefully plan informal gatherings outside of school in order to facilitate more personal relationships.

Collaborative Goal Setting

If you don't know where you're going, how can you get there? As co-teachers, we plan together, teach together, assess together, and we also set goals together. We define collaborative goal setting as deciding on our intentions as a team. In general, goal setting can foster professional growth and development, but collaborative goals also provide the why of our collaboration. The beginning of any new school year is an ideal time to sit down to discuss and develop mutual goals, but we don't stop there. We visit and analyze the progress of our goals together often. Developing these goals together as collaborators is crucial to ensuring dual ownership over our agreed-upon objectives as a team. There is no special formula for how many goals you should set or any particular format. For us, we set three measurable goals: one focusing on **co-teaching** and/or **collaboration** (CT and/or C), one focusing on our **professional (teaching) practice** (PP), and one focusing on **student performance** and achievement (STP). You and your collaborator(s) will have to decide together what type of goals you want to set and what they will be.

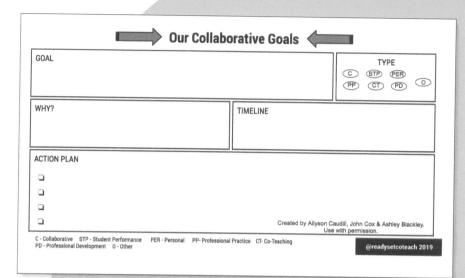

Figure 4A: Collaborative Goal-Setting Worksheet for setting collaborative goals with one or more collaborators.

Sample Collaborative Goals @readysetcoach 2019

Collaborative (C) Goal: We will record at least one glow and one grows in our reflection journals daily and share them once a week.

Professional Practice (PP) Goal: We will incorporate at least 3 different student interaction strategies in our lesson each week.

Student Performance (STP) Goal: By the end of the unit, at least 80% of our students will score a 3 or above in the summative assessment.

Figure 4B: Collaborative goals we have set for ourselves in the past.

SWIRLing in the Content Areas

At the core of our practice is the incorporation of both receptive (listening, reading) and productive (speaking, writing) language skills into every content lesson by adapting the curriculum, tasks, and expectations. Language is embedded into every subject and is paramount in learning academic content, but in a certain sense, as Bourdieu et al. (1994) assert, "Academic language is…no one's mother tongue" (p. 8).

Accordingly, when we sit down to collaborate and plan our language-rich content lessons, one of our goals is to incorporate multiple opportunities for students to use targeted academic language in all four domains: speaking, writing, reading, and listening (SWRL), through meaningful interactions (I) with their peers. When applied to instructional practices, this is known as SWIRLing. Focusing on cultivating a SWIRLing classroom when planning instruction ensures teachers design activities that engage students in speaking, writing, peer interaction, reading, and listening in every lesson. In this way, English learners not only learn about the English language, but they also learn content through English, so we write both content and language objectives for every lesson with a SWIRLing classroom in mind. The content objective is directly related to the key concept of the lesson based on the content standards and curriculum. In contrast, the language objective promotes students' academic language growth by articulating for learners the academic language functions and skills they need to master in order to fully participate in the lesson (Echevarría, Vogt, & Short, 2017). Both native English speakers and language learners alike can benefit from the intentional co-planning of SWIRLing activities that support language development through academic tasks.

STRATEGIES FOR SWIRLing IN THE CONTENT AREAS				
Speaking	**W**riting	**I**nteraction	**R**eading	**L**istening
• Sentence frames • Conversation cues • Talk moves • Equity sticks • Talking chips • Role playing • Established discussion norms • Word banks	• Shared writing • Sentence & paragraph frames • Word banks • Visual supports • Color-coding & checklists • Talk, Read, Talk, Write (Motley, 2016)	• Strategic grouping • Flexible grouping • Back-to-back, face-to-face • Collaborative pairs • Think-Pair-Share	• Explicitly teach phonics & phonemic awareness skills • Front load essential vocabulary • Analyze text • Teach text features • Reader's Theater • Repeated, shared and choral reading • Chunk & summarize	• Comprehensible input • Podcasts • Second set partners • Read-alouds & think-alouds

Wait Time • Modeling • Graphic Organizers • Multiple Choice
Rubrics • Visual Supports (illustrations, photographs, etc) • Manipulatives & Realia
Charts, Tables, & Graphs • Interactive Word Walls • Graphic Organizers

Figure 5A. Chart showing suggested strategies to fold language into content through SWIRL
Created by Allyson Caudill, John Cox & Ashley Blackley. Used with permission.

PLANNING FOR LANGUAGE INTEGRATION RESOURCE

This organizer is a great tool for identifying and addressing the language needs of instructional activities and tasks. Adapted from Wake County Public Schools Academic Language Department.

PLANNING FOR LANGUAGE INTEGRATION

Topic 1st Grade Math: Place Value

Speaking and Listening Goal	**Content Specific Goal**
Build on others' talk by responding to the comments of others through multiple exchanges.	Recognize and name the value of the digits in a 2-digit number.

Activity
Students will name the value of the underlined digit in a two-digit number.

Example: 5̲2. The value of the 5 in 52 is 50.

Grouping Strategy	**Interaction Strategy**
____Partners _x_ Triads ____Small Group ____Other: _____	**Campfire** - Students sit in groups of three with the activity in the middle like a campfire. The students are each assigned a job. **Talker** - Shares the card and what they think the value is for the underlined digit and expand on why using the sentence frame. **Listener** - Paraphrases when the talker is finished and responds appropriately using the conversation cues. **Observer** - Observes both the talker and listener and watches for conversation norms using a checklist. The observer gives feedback to both the talker and listener at the end of the activity.

Scaffolds & Supports
- **Sentence Frames** (The value of _____ in the number _____ is ___ because ___.)
- **Conversation Cues** (I agree, I disagree, I would like to add on/clarify/ask a question)
- **Discussion Norms & Rubric**
- **Manipulatives & Graphic Organizer** (Place Value Mat)

Figure 5C. Completed Planning for Language Integration Resource
Sample organizer completed collaboratively by Allyson and Ashley.
Adapted from Wake County Public Schools Academic Language Department.

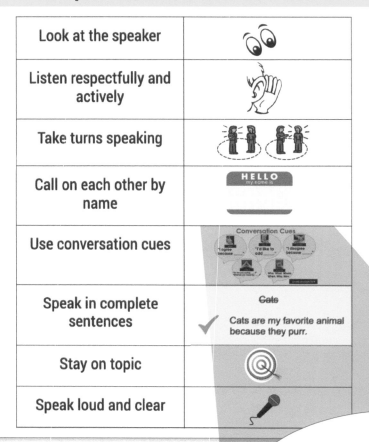

Sample Classroom Discussion Norms

Look at the speaker	
Listen respectfully and actively	
Take turns speaking	
Call on each other by name	
Use conversation cues	
Speak in complete sentences	~~Cats~~ ✓ Cats are my favorite animal because they purr.
Stay on topic	
Speak loud and clear	

Figure 5E.
Sample Classroom Discussion Norms Created by Allyson Caudill, John Cox & Ashley Blackley.
Used with permission.

Sample Conversation Cues

AGREE "I agree because _____"

ADD ON "I'd like to add _____."

DISAGREE "I disagree because _____."

CLARIFY "So are you saying _____?" "What do you mean by _____?"

QUESTION Who, What, Where, When, Why, How

Figure 5D. Sample Conversation Cues Created by Allyson Caudill, John Cox & Ashley Blackley. Used with permission.

STUDENT SUCCESS STORIES

Meet Isaac
(Six years old, native Spanish speaker, from Honduras)

Isaac joined our co-taught first-grade class about two months after school started. He got along great with his classmates, participated fully (whether in English or Spanish), and always did his best. He was a wonderful addition to our classroom family, but we were concerned with his academics. He was reading at a beginning kindergarten level (RB)* and, since he came to us two months in, had missed a good chunk of instruction. We immediately began working to support him in building his confidence and collaborated to set up a plan to make the content accessible to him while also growing his language proficiency. Since we co-teach, we were able to provide two small group sessions with a teacher per day—one with Ashley that focused on explicit phonics instruction and the other with Allyson focusing on the language of the curriculum and strategies to be successful. Each time we co-planned for whole group instruction and independent work, we strategically chose scaffolds and supports that would meet his needs (as well as the needs of other students). For example, for every writing task, we provided word banks and sentence frames. We used an increased number of visuals in every lesson and made sure to pre-plan and pre-teach Tier 2 vocabulary using visuals and gestures to elicit meaning. We also had crucial conversations about how Ashley could integrate language supports into her math block when Allyson wasn't there.

Before we knew it, Isaac was making substantial growth. He jumped right into assignments, soaking up everything he could. His effort went through the roof because he felt he could be successful. By the time he moved onto the co-taught second-grade class with John and Allyson, he was reading and comprehending on a level L, which means he grew 12 reading levels in less than one year. But he didn't stop there. During the summer before he moved up to second grade, we met as a triad. Ashley and Allyson shared with John all the strategies that worked for him, and we all brainstormed ways to continue to push him forward. During his second grade year with John and Allyson, he expanded his learning by taking more of a leadership role and becoming a model for others. He was not only effectively using scaffolds, he was also teaching others and even created the sentence frames for the class during various activities. Over the course of the year, he grew four more reading levels and increased his WIDA language proficiency level to a 5 (Bridging)!

*Reading Behaviors - as defined by North Carolina Reading Level Expectations

Meet Ali

(Eight years old, Spanish speaker, born in the U.S., family is Salvadoran)

We first met Ali three years ago when she was in a neighboring teacher's first-grade class. Allyson did her best to meet Ali's language needs through a scheduled ESL pull-out group and by supporting her classroom teacher as needed. Unfortunately, it wasn't enough, and Ali struggled in literacy. After several conversations among her teacher, Allyson, her parents, and our principal, the decision was made to keep Ali in first grade for an additional year. With that decision came questions about how we could change what we were doing to ensure Ali was successful the second time around. We all agreed to move her into the co-taught first-grade room (Ashley and Allyson's) to see if that environment would make a difference. Ali is soft-spoken, shy, and needed encouragement to come out of her shell. She loved her previous first-grade teacher and had built a great relationship with her, so we always looked to that teacher for tips and kept her updated on Ali's progress.

Before the year began, Ashley and Allyson sat down to discuss how we could create an environment in which Ali would feel safe and motivated to take risks. We strategically paired her with a fluent English-speaking peer who we thought would be a great model during collaborative work but wouldn't overpower her. We spent the year tracking Ali's progress in all areas and adjusted our instruction to fill in the gaps and meet her needs based on our findings. We tagged fluency and comprehension as her biggest obstacles. By dissecting the content together and anticipating challenges, Ashley and Allyson were able to develop scaffolds that allowed Ali to access the content and continue growing. Slowly but surely, Ali was able to interact with her peers without needing all the support provided by the scaffolds. By the end of the year, Ali had surpassed grade-level expectations and grown her reading level from a C to a K: eight levels.

This year Ali is in John and Allyson's co-taught second-grade class. We continue to work on building her confidence, but her academics haven't faltered. We have implemented the strategies that worked for Ali last year but have also collaboratively developed more based on the second grade curriculum and expectations. Ali does especially well when given sufficient wait time, an academic word wall she constantly uses as a word bank, sentence frames, and conversation cues she can use when sharing with the whole class. By providing these supports, we are working to instill confidence in Ali to participate in class discussions. Ali has learned that her voice has value in our classroom, and we will continue to provide support and positive reinforcement to cement that lesson. Ali has twin younger siblings who are now in Ashley and Allyson's first-grade room. All three of us (Allyson, John, and Ashley) have built a close-knit relationship with the family, and their parents come on almost every field trip.

●●● CONCLUSION

The moral of our collaboration story is this: Our team has a more positive impact on student achievement together than we ever did individually. Effective collaboration takes time, effort, and trust, but when it is achieved, the outcomes can be extraordinary for students and teachers alike. But don't take it from us; listen to our students. Here were their responses last year when we asked what they liked about having two teachers:

I like having two teachers because...

I get more hugs every day.
– Blessing, Age 8

They teach us different things.
– Allison, Age 7

Two is better than one.
– Stephie, Age 7

I have more help. – Kaylie, Age 8

When one teacher is absent, the other teacher can take over. – Jefferson, Age 9

I like going to two tables.
– Nathan, Age 6 (in reference to reading groups)

My two teachers help each other. – Devin, Age 7

I can do more with two teachers. – Isha, Age 7

I get more attention. – Sayuri, Age 6

If a kid needs help and then another kid does too, it's great to have two teachers because there are two teachers that can help. – Sophia, Age 6

You can learn more. – Ella, Age 6

If you have two teachers, one can take care of a group, and the other teacher can take care of another group so all kids can be learning at one time. – Gage, Age 6

If someone needs help, the other teacher can keep teaching.
– Ian, Age 6

Collaborative Lesson Plan

John and Allyson
ELA Q1- Topic: Schools and Community

Essential Question(s):
How are schools different around the world? How are they similar?

Key Content Vocabulary
compare   both   alike   similar contrast   but   same   different
Read-Aloud Vocab (Tier II)
From "Schools that Go to Kids" (pp. 50–51 of *Off to Class*) - obstacles, slum, laborer, doorstep, pace, admission

Topic Schools and Community	**Task** Comparing and Contrasting: High Quality Sentences
Targets I can compare and contrast my own school with a different school. I can respond to others' ideas while participating in a collaborative conversation about similarities in the schools we have researched. W2.2, W2.5, L2.2	Texts *Off to Class: Incredible and Unusual Schools around the World*

Standard(s): SL 2.1, W 2.8, RI 2.1 2.7

Language Objective(s): We can compare and contrast two different schools in complete sentences in an informational book. We will use sentence frames, conversation cues, writing partners, and modeling to help us.

	Lesson Activities	Teacher Duties	Supports
Module 1, Unit 2, Lesson 8	• Reader's Theater video (10 mins) • Intro to reading with expression - sentence strips • Ruby with Allyson and Quartz with John. Emerald and Sapphire read to self the scripts (p. 200) (10 mins) • Boat Group: D, K, J, M, J, A • Amazon Group: J, B, L, D, J, S • Earthquake Group: M, I, S, C, F, J, K • Rehearse with groups (20 mins) • Feedback on how the collaboration went (whole group)	Allyson Criteria and expectations checklist, reading with expression sentence strips (cut & put in bag) John Reader's Theater script copies - highlight parts	• Video example • Modeling • Strategic grouping **Conversation cues** Sentence frames for feedback: *One thing our group did well was _____.* *One thing our group can do better next time is _____.*

Figure 3. Example of Collaboratively Planned Lesson. Example ELA lesson co-planned by John and Allyson that includes annotated language supports to meet the needs of all students.

Module 1, Unit 2, Lesson 9	• Review criteria and expectations (5 mins) • Turn & Talk for two scenarios (10 mins) • Rehearse for 15 mins • Reader's Theater performances (20 mins) • Reflection - reviewing module guiding questions to wrap up unit	Allyson Criteria handouts John	• Criteria and expectations checklists • Turn & Talk for scenarios • Sentence frame for Turn & Talk: *In this scenario I would _____ because _____.* • Conversation cues • Practice/rehearsal time
Module 1, Unit 3, Lesson 1	• Intro compare and contrast anchor chart and color coding • New word wall words: differences, similarities, contrast, compare, build on, collaborative • 3-school organizer reviewing boat school • Fill in facts today about only boat school • Think, pair, share contrast sentences • Students write contrast sentences • Think, pair, share compare sentences • Students write compare sentences • Share sentence with a random partner, practicing adding on • Wrap-up by having kids share out sentences	Allyson Copies of 3-school anchor chart, word wall word cards John Post compare/contrast anchor chart	• Compare (blue) and contrast (red) color-coded anchor chart with sentence frames • Think, pair, share • Conversation cues • 3-school graphic organizer • Chunking (only boat school today) • Gestures during read-aloud (when Ss hear a similarity both hands together, a difference hands far apart) • Word wall (with visuals and meanings)

References and Further Resources

Bourdieu, P., Passeron, J-C., & Saint Martin, M. (1994). *Academic discourse: Linguistic misunderstanding and professorial power.* Polity.

Caudill, A., Cox, J., & Blackley, A. (n.d.). *Ready, Set, Co-Teach!* http://www.readysetcoteach.com/

Dove, M. G., & Honigsfeld, A. (2018). *Co-teaching for English learners: A guide to collaborative planning, instruction, assessment, and reflection.* Corwin.

Echevarría, J., Vogt, M. E., & Short, D. (2017). *Making content comprehensible for English learners: The SIOP model.* Pearson.

Fisher, D., Frey, N., & Rothenberg, C. (2008). *Content-area conversations: How to plan discussion-based lessons for diverse language learners.* Association for Supervision and Curriculum Development.

Hattie, J. (2009). *Visible learning: A synthesis of over 800 meta-analyses relating to achievement.* Routledge.

Honigsfeld, A., & Dove, M. G. (2019). *Collaborating for English learners: A foundational guide to integrated practices.* Corwin.

Motley, N. (2016). *Talk, Read, Talk, Write: A practical routine for learning in all content areas (K-12).* Seidlitz Education.

WIDA. (2014). *Collaborative learning for English language learners.* https://wida.wisc.edu/sites/default/files/resource/Brief-CollaborativeLearningforELLs.pdf

WIDA. (2021). *ACCESS for ELLs.* https://wida.wisc.edu/assess/access

2

Pushing
the Boundaries
of Collaboration

Carmen O'Brien and
Brittany Schmidt

SNAPSHOT

Carmen O'Brien and Brittany Schmidt
are seventh grade English language arts
teachers at Greenville Middle School in Greenville,
WI. Greenville Middle School is situated in a rural
community and serves 680 students in grades 5
through 8. Carmen has been teaching for six years
and Brittany for ten years, yet this was only their
second year team teaching together. Both teachers
are certified to teach English learners (ELs). They are
passionate about meeting the needs of all learners as
well as building their students' love for reading and
writing. As they enter their third year of team teaching,
they have the unique situation of having English as a
Second Language (ESL) backgrounds and experience,
while at the same time working as English Language
Arts (ELA) content teachers.

"Many ideas grow better
when transplanted into another
mind than the one where they
sprang up."
- OLIVER WENDELL HOLMES

SETTING THE STAGE

We are not traditional team teachers or co-teachers—we tend to use these terms synonymously. Our class is not the typical setup of one core content teacher and one specialist in one class-room. Instead, we are both dual-certified to teach ELA and ESL. Our unique way of co-teaching is what makes our combined classroom special. Team teaching has not only made us better teachers but has made our ideas stronger by putting our minds together. There are endless ways to collaborate with the goal of develop-ing independent, resilient, and confident learners. We have been collaborating in ways that have pushed our thinking and, in turn, have influenced others' ideas and beliefs. In this chapter, we want to share how we have pushed the boundaries of our collaboration and why we think it has yielded such positive outcomes.

When we found out we would be collabo-rating as teaching partners, it was as if a million light bulbs went off in our minds. Our separate classrooms are joined by a retractable wall, and while some may look at that situation with caution and unease, we only saw the opportunities it would bring. Even though we are bringing two classrooms together as one, we have ownership of both classes. All the students in seventh grade ELA are our students. We don't see two classrooms. We see one large learning community.

Getting Started

The first week of school is dedicated to building relationships and getting to know our students, so we have the wall between our classrooms up, and our classes remain separate. After that first week, the wall is seldom up, and our two classes become one. The seventh graders look at both of us as their ELA teachers. With our class being double the size of a regular class, our co-planning time is not just essential; it is sacred. Organization and comprehen-sive planning are a must when thinking about the management and success of 56 students at a time. Don't let that number scare you. Trust us, we've heard all the doubts:

> *"There is no way you can make sure that many students are on task."*

> *"How can you check for understanding with all of those students?"*

> *"It's impossible to manage the behavior of so many middle schoolers."*

> *"That is not co-teaching!"*

We are here to say that, when co-teaching is approached as a trusting partnership, with each teacher having a collaborative, in-it-together mindset, the right intentions, and the ability to adapt and be flexible on the spot, the number of students in the room does not matter.

When we sit down to plan together, we come to the table with our strengths and challenges. One of us is a stronger reading teacher, and the other is a stronger writing teacher. We both have skills to contribute and ideas to offer. During a planning session, we consider multiple factors: students identified as ELs and/or for special education services, students reading at various levels, behavior combinations, seating preferences, etc. All of our lessons take into account the different modalities of learning and, as such, appeal to the unique learners in our class. Depending on the co-teaching model we use on a given day, one of us will be observing behaviors and assessing students while the other is leading the lesson. Based on those observations, we have a better idea of what the students know and what we need to change in order for them to better understand the content. This practice makes us more reflective and better teachers because we are able to adapt at any given moment.

By our second year collaborating with a combined classroom, we were making more and more changes to our lesson plans and units to better suit the diverse needs of our students. While we always have had our ELs and students identified as needing special education services in mind when planning, we had more students during our second year who struggled behaviorally, socially, and emotionally, which brought in extra challenges to consider.

BLUEPRINT

To succeed as a collaborative team, we follow a collaborative instructional and assessment cycle—co-planning, co-teaching, co-assessment, and reflection. Maria Dove and Andrea Honigsfeld (2018) note, "We strongly concur that there is an urgent need to look beyond the instructional classroom practices of co-teaching. Ignoring three elements of the collaborative cycle—co-planning, co-assessment, and reflection—would significantly disrupt the instructional balance and negatively impact student learning" (p. xi). All four parts of this cycle are crucial in the success of our collaboration and of our students, so we consider the following questions in our work:

1. How do we collaboratively plan?
2. How do we co-teach in a collaborative environment?
3. How do we co-assess?
4. How do we reflect in order to grow as a collaborative partnership?

Throughout this next section, we will answer these four essential questions in depth.

Collaborative Planning

When we sit down to plan collaboratively, we always start with the end in mind. We look at the learning target for the following week and break it into daily mini-lessons, each with a guiding principle. For example, the learning target for one week may be, "I can identify the key characteristics of a memoir and provide textual evidence to support my thinking." We would divide this objective into the principles of the three key characteristics of a memoir—the significant time/place/event, the author's feelings, and factual information about the author. We would then split each principle into the appropriate number of days it should take to teach and determine how to best deliver instruction, considering mentor texts, short videos, new texts, and other mediums. During this time, we would also consider the different needs of our students and our specific roles as co-teachers for each lesson—who will model, who will observe student learning, who will read aloud, and so on.

All of our ideas for differentiating do not necessarily happen at the moment we are sitting down to plan out the week, however. We usually come back the next day (after we have absorbed all of the different ideas) and decide how we should actually co-deliver and scaffold instruction. Figure 1 shows our lesson planning template with a sample differentiated lesson.

Date: 12-12-19

SEL Objective: *I can reflect on possible consequences, both positive and negative, before expressing an emotion or behavior.*

Content Objective: *I can research a time period to create an authentic Historical Fiction narrative.*

Language Objective: *I can read an independent Historical Fiction book and listen to a Historical Fiction read aloud to gain an understanding of different time periods and authentic details. I can write a Historical Fiction narrative.*

TEACHER 1 ROLE	TEACHER 2 ROLE
Read aloud chapters 20-23 in Between Shades of Gray.	During the read aloud, add words/phrases to our ongoing list of authentic language, and add problem and/or rising action to our ongoing plot map.
Model how we took notes in our research guide using the time period of the 1800s.	Using what Teacher 1 says in her notes, begin drawing our main character and filling in possible internal/external conflicts.
Confer with individual students on their research.	Confer with individual students on their research.

Planning for **Differentiation**:

English Learners	Special Education	Tier II
Prepare a word list of authentic language in The Boy in the Striped Pajamas. Build background knowledge of the "Fury" by watching a short video on Hitler and the Nazis. Point out how their new home is referred to as "Out With" and read an article together on Auschwitz. Set up a double entry journal with information on Auschwitz on the left, and comparing/contrasting that information with Bruno's perspective on the right.	The special education teacher will take the Number the Stars group and read aloud another chapter while they follow along. He will stop occasionally to model how to keep a running list of authentic language to the time period and explain how he knows they are authentic words/phrases. Students will copy these words/phrases down in their notebooks.	Provide identity cards of Holocaust survivors to help personally connect to characters in both The Boy in the Striped Pajamas and Number the Stars. Students may use one of the identify cards to help develop their main character in their narrative.

Observed behaviors (during):
Reflection (after):
- How will we support observed behaviors?
- How did the lesson go? What will we keep or change?
- Next steps

Figure 1

During our second year of co-teaching, we noticed our plans for writing units often changed on a daily basis. This was a red flag. For us, the changes signaled an inability to stick to a plan, or possible ineffective planning, which meant that last minute changes were necessary. We also realized that the lack of consistency was hindering our students' comprehension and grasp of writing skills. We saw that they struggled with working independently and did not demonstrate confidence in their ideas. So, to develop writing stamina and to promote independent writers, we began creating student-friendly, interactive checklists.

These checklists have helped all of our students tremendously by laying out clear, step-by-step expectations that are easily accessible and by guiding students to what is needed to master the essential learning standards. They have also improved the way we confer with students during independent writing time because we know we're working with a well-designed scaffold based on the expertise of multiple teachers.

Introduction Checklist

Hook

☐ Strong statement

☐ Compelling fact or statistic

☐ Quote

☐ Metaphor/Simile

Background
Does your background info:

☐ Prepare your readers to explore a topic further?

☐ Enable your readers to predict what is to come next?

☐ Show your readers the significance of the topic presented?

Thesis Statement
Is it:

☐ Clear and specific?

☐ A central idea/message?

☐ The topic of your essay?

☐ Original?

☐ Stated to avoid a universal structure? (I.e., not, "My thesis is..." or "The topic of my paper is...")

Personal Essay Drafting Checklist

Intro
- ☐ Hook
- ☐ Background
- ☐ Thesis

Body Paragraph 1
- ☐ Topic: _____
- ☐ Anecdote or Information
- ☐ Topic elaborated in a few sentences
- ☐ Source cited (if applicable)

Body Paragraph 2
- ☐ Topic: _____
- ☐ Anecdote or Information
- ☐ Topic elaborated in a few sentences
- ☐ Source cited (if applicable)

Body Paragraph 3
- ☐ Topic: _____
- ☐ Anecdote or Information
- ☐ Topic elaborated in a few sentences
- ☐ Source cited (if applicable)

Conclusion
- ☐ Restates thesis in a new way
- ☐ Restates main points (topics of each body paragraph)
- ☐ Makes lasting impression on reader

Did I
- ☐ Include at least two pieces of information and cite each piece?
- ☐ Give this my **best** effort?

Before we even began co-teaching, we knew we would work well together, but even we had adjustments to make. Just as our students may experience the stages of culture shock in a new environment, co-teachers can as well. Rachel Irwin (2007) describes culture shock as "the anxiety and emotional disturbance experienced by people when two sets of realities and conceptualisations meet" (para. 2). This aligns perfectly with our situation of two classrooms, two separate realities, coming together as one. As co-teachers, we have experienced these stages of culture shock, as shown in Figure 2.

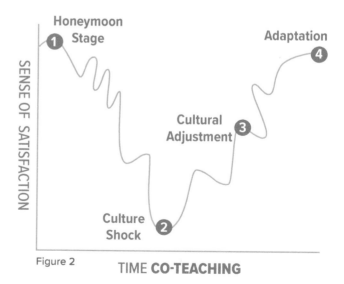

Figure 2

It is imperative to note that a co-teaching partnership cannot be forced. It takes time to adjust, especially if it is your first experience in a collaborative environment. We have spent most of our current partnership of two years in the "honeymoon stage," with only these minor culture shocks to overcome. We have been excited about this journey from the start, and that excitement about collaborating and combining our classes has not gone away. We know that while some of the initial shine of these early years may eventually fade, we will only continue to grow more effective the longer we are able to refine our skills together. Students have even commented on how much fun we have together, saying they love being in a class where their teachers are happy and have fun with them.

The group of students we had during our second year co-teaching together were extremely different from the first, and we were challenged in new ways. We had to be more strategic in planning for and applying class management strategies compared with planning for students' academic needs. With this in mind and our growing class sizes, some may doubt how combining our classes was best for kids. However, more problems arose when we were separated into two classes than when we were together as one. This was due to our careful planning of how we would be co-teaching each lesson and our ability to maintain the excitement and joy in our co-taught classroom. We weren't just teaching every day; we were having fun! When students saw us having fun, they realized that it was okay for them to have fun too.

Co-Teaching

A Typical Lesson: After thoughtful and intentional planning, we felt prepared to be successful in co-teaching. We began each lesson together with an attention grabber—something to hook students' interest. Once students were engaged, we transitioned into our mini-lesson. It was critical that our mini-lessons were no longer than 10 to 12 minutes. Teacher 1, who served as the lead teacher for the mini-lesson, did the instructing and would sometimes model as well. Sometimes Teacher 2 would model instead, using the document camera as Teacher 1 narrated.

Following the mini-lesson, students began their independent work time. This was the most important component, and it took up the majority of our blocked class time (45 to 60 minutes). Before going into each day, we had already planned which teacher would work with which students. On a typical day, one teacher worked with our targeted groups—Tier II students, or those not making adequate progress in the core curriculum, students with special needs, and English learners. The other conferred with the rest of the students, either individually or in strategy groups. We tried to work with our targeted groups once a day, and we conferred with students performing at or above grade level once a week.

Students in our targeted groups typically needed more examples of how to apply the skill from the mini-lesson. During the mini-lesson, we used grade-level texts to model, but sometimes we used a lower-level text to model the concept again with a targeted group. We also had students practice with a shared text because we have found that students in these targeted groups would rather read with a partner or follow along with a teacher than read independently. Having a shared text allowed this group to make more connections, and we felt confident that students were applying the strategies we taught them to their reading. In writing, we offered these students sentence starters and were more explicit about how to structure their writing. We also frequently utilized Thinking Maps as tools for students to plan out their writing before drafting. Since students were familiar with Thinking Maps—they are up in our classroom most of the time—these tools were also excellent resources to use with our targeted groups to focus students on a particular task or explicitly teach a writing skill.

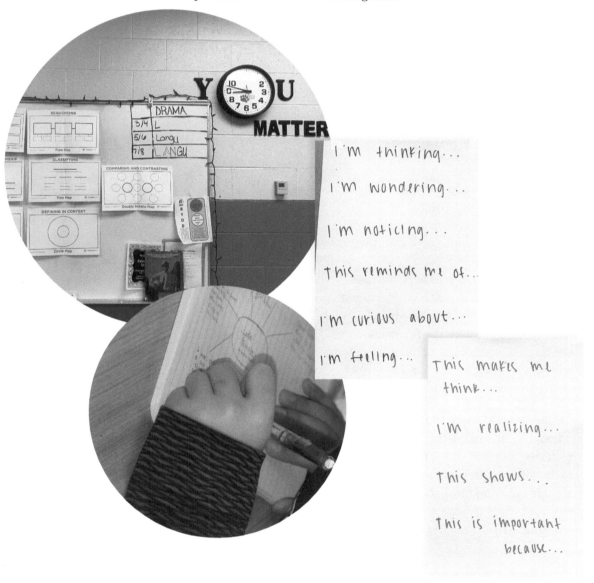

I'm thinking...

I'm wondering...

I'm noticing...

This reminds me of...

I'm curious about...

I'm feeling...

This makes me think...

I'm realizing...

This shows...

This is important because...

As mentioned previously, we meet individually with students at or above grade level once a week. During this conference time, the teacher, in collaboration with the student, selects a goal for the student to work on based on what either notices about the student's reading or writing. Both then record this goal so that they can revisit it to see the student's progress at the next conference. If the student reaches that goal, the teacher and student work together to create another one. Both of us shared the details of these student meetings with each other because we switch daily to work with students in turn. In order to share this data, we have found it best to keep binders to record information—one for the target groups and one for the individual conferences.

Our lessons generally end with a share out. This final lesson component is an opportunity for students to share what they accomplished during independent work time. Additionally, if a student has demonstrated the targeted skill well, we may show the rest of the class. While students are sharing, we create a list of students we want to check in with the following day. We can tell who needs a little more attention based on either the students' work or the conversations they are having.

Co-Teaching Models: While we are creative in arranging our shared space with two teachers in the combined classroom, we have found three co-teaching models to be the most effective: station teaching, team teaching, and parallel teaching.

Station teaching is something we use often with our combined classroom because it offers differentiation, small group teacher support, movement, and engagement. Typically, when we are on a station rotation day, we offer two teacher-guided groups that focus on a specific skill, an independent reading/writing station, an online learning tool, and a mini-lesson application station. We strategically group our students for the teacher-led station to differentiate for their needs. Some students require the preteaching or reteaching of certain skills to reach mastery, whereas other students who have met the benchmark are provided with enrichment activities.

A day of station teaching begins with a regular ten-minute mini-lesson. After the mini-lesson, we typically explain what students will be doing at each station. Once everyone is clear on directions, we display the rotation schedule for the day and remind students where each will begin. Usually, our students who are independent learners with good time management skills are placed in the mini-lesson application stations first. This way, our students who need more guided practice can benefit from the teacher-led stations before they apply what they have learned independently.

Team teaching is the model we are most comfortable with as a partnership. In this model, all of the students come together for the mini-lesson, the students in one of our classrooms staying in their seats while the others come over and sit on the mat. In a typical mini-lesson, one teacher will read a mentor text while the other either discusses her thinking or models a skill students will be applying during independent reading. In a writing mini-lesson, we typically bounce ideas off of each other while we model our thinking as writers to students.

Video:
Team Teaching
in Action

We feel extremely fortunate to have the co-teaching partnership we do. We find that we often finish each other's sentences or ideas and expand on each other's thinking. One of our favorite units to team teach is our book club. During this unit, we model what an effective book club looks like and what academic language sounds like during book discussions. Sometimes we will do a fishbowl discussion in which pairs or small groups of students engage in conversations while other students listen. Other times, we model discussions in our mini-lessons.

When we are team teaching, we do not have to designate who will say what or when one of us will jump in; it happens as a result of our balanced partnership and our shared agency to seize a teachable moment. We know where we want our students to be, so each of us is free to spontaneously add to the discussion during instruction to get them there. There is no frustration with one of us speaking more than the other. Our partnership is not a competition. It is part of the trust we have built as co-teachers, and one of the ways we teach that our students are most familiar with.

Parallel teaching is the model we use most often in the beginning of the year. We begin each day as a combined class for the mini-lesson, and then we break up into our read-aloud groups. Each group has the same focus as the mini-lesson, but how we get there may look different. Once we are situated in our read-aloud groups (which are mixed groups from both classes), the wall is closed, and we can differentiate based on each group's needs.

One way we have used parallel teaching is to prepare for Socratic seminars. One of us takes our fluent, grade-level or above readers who are comfortable with their communication skills, and the other takes our emergent or early fluent readers who may need to further develop their speaking and listening skills. While we both guide the annotation process and prepare for our first discussion, we may be tackling different skills or annotating for various text elements. The texts we use in our groups are also differentiated. With our different groups during parallel teaching, we focus in more detail on speaking and listening skills. We developed a rubric that we use to prepare and assess the speaking and listening skills of our students when we conduct activities such as a Socratic seminar. Figure 3 shows the behaviors and skills we target in different ways and at different paces in our parallel teaching groups.

Co-Assessment

We also calibrate our grading as co-teachers in our content-area PLC. After summatively assessing a standard, we sit down

I can respond to questions with elaboration and detail that connect with what is being discussed. Socratic Seminar			
Not Yet (1)	**Near Mastery (2)**	**Mastery (3)**	**Exceeds (4)**
• Has not prepared or asked questions • Disruptive or silent • Attempts to dominate, or interrupts speakers • Unprepared or unfamiliar with the text	• Has prepared/asks very few questions, if any • Addresses only the teacher, ideas do not always connect • Loses track of conversations, judges others' ideas • Very few notes, if any	• Has prepared questions and asks some during seminar • Comments often, refers to the text, responds to questions • Eye contact with speakers, positive body language • Prepared notes and annotations	• Has prepared five or more high level questions and asks several during seminar • Moves conversation forward, makes connections to other speakers • Demonstrates active listening, builds on others' comments, asks for clarification • Prepared many notes and annotations

Figure 3

together, go through several individual student assessments, and discuss where each student would fall on the rubric. Once we feel confident that we are on the same page, we continue with the students on our own rosters in order to be timely and efficient. If any questions arise, we tackle them together.

It is important for us to tackle assessments as a partnership so that we can make notes on what we need to reteach and decide which students may benefit from enrichment. This co-assessment process provides us with opportunities to place students strategically in station groups and design lessons to engage our various learners. In other words, co-assessment is an essential part of co-planning.

One aspect of co-assessment that has been a huge part of our combined class during our second year of teaching together is our consideration of Tier II students. Our building identifies Tier II students as those who have scored in the 40th percentile in STAR reading for the past three assessments as well as scoring Below Basic on the Forward Exam. During our second year co-teaching, we had 28 seventh graders identified as Tier II in reading. Due to this large group requiring targeted intervention, we had to become extremely

mindful and strategic in looking at our data to plan instruction for this time.

Recently, we have utilized our school-wide intervention time, WIN, to co-teach a month-long Tier II reading intervention group. To organize this group, we selected 20 seventh graders who had been identified as Tier II. For each of these 20 students, we created data tracking sheets for each student to record STAR progress monitoring scores, Read Theory data (a web-based reading comprehension program), and reading stamina goals and behaviors.

Each week had the same structure for this WIN group—reading a new short story

Name:

Read Theory

Date	# of quizzes taken today	# of quizzes passed today	Knowledge Point Total	Program Average

STAR

Date	Scaled Score (SS)	Percentile Rank (PR)

Reading Stamina

Date	Time Read	Focus Level (1-10)

together and talking about the text. To model how this activity should look, one of us would read a section out loud and then the other would think out loud using the sentence stems "I'm noticing," "I'm wondering," or "I'm thinking." After each of us modeled our thinking, we would invite some students to share their thinking for the group. While students gave voice to their ideas, other students listened and jotted down notes in the margins of their short story. The next day would be a day to reread the short story and annotate for unknown words, foreshadowing, and high-level questioning. Wednesdays were dedicated to personalized learning and progress monitoring using Read Theory. On Thursdays, we would revisit the short story and make inferences, which we had identified as a challenging and necessary reading skill. And on Fridays, we would end the week by building independent reading stamina.

Reflection

Reflection is an ongoing process that is often done in the moment. We generally adapt what we will be doing from one lesson block to the next. Flexibility and trust are vital components in our partnership and are on full display when reflection happens between classes. We are usually on the same page when one of us hints that the lesson is not going as well as planned. Often when this happens, one of us jumps in with an idea about how we can improve for the next block.

In our district, we value participation in professional learning communities (PLCs). In our PLCs, we constantly reflect and

Find out more about "All Things PLC" by Solution Tree.

evaluate ourselves as educators using Rick DuFour et al.'s (2006) four essential PLC questions:

- **What do we want each student to learn?**
- **How will we know when each student has learned it?**
- **How will we respond when they don't learn?**
- **How will we respond if they already know it?**

As co-teachers, we utilize the three big ideas of a PLC as outlined by Solution Tree (2021). We (a) focus on learning, (b) build a collaborative culture, and (c) focus on results. Based on these ideals, we have developed our collaboration to be ongoing, constant, and purposeful.

Reflection also occurs after school, when we modify our plans for the following day based on student performance and our observations. We include a reflection portion in our lesson planning template (see p. 35) in which we think about our daily lessons. We begin reflecting on our observations of student performance for that day and determine how we can mitigate the behaviors that hindered student success. Then we generalize how the overall lesson went and discuss whether students have met the objective of the day. We revisit our planned-out lessons for the week and determine if we need to change anything or keep it as is. Finally, our next steps include identifying what we will do differently or deciding if we should keep our plans for the following day. All of our reflection revolves around students. It truly is a day-to-day process, which is why flexibility and trust in each other are key.

HIGH IMPACT STRATEGIES

Though our use of a collaborative instruction and assessment cycle is nothing new, there are four areas within our co-taught classroom in which we push the boundaries of our favorite co-teaching models: class size, social-emotional learning, differentiation of instruction, and conferring with students. We have developed strategies, routines, and beliefs in these four areas that make them highly impactful. We recognize that our situation is distinctly unique from those of other teachers; nevertheless, this is what has worked for us.

Pushing the Boundaries on Class Size

If there is strength in numbers, our classroom is the most powerful indeed. Every human being has multiple strengths. With our classroom consisting of 56 students at any given time, just thinking about all the potential there is mind-blowing.

Matthew Lynch (2017) claims that "small class sizes work because they give teachers an opportunity to offer students more personalized instruction" (para. 4). And yet, with our large combined class, we see even more opportunities for personalized instruction because there are more peers at each instructional level for students to interact with. We are always meticulous in our planning with this many students and are extremely aware of how we will meet the needs of every single one. We still hold high expectations that all students are working with rigorous grade-level content, but some groups will need different instructional paths to meet a standard. This number of students makes planning for station teaching more meaningful—and easier—since we can have appropriately large group sizes for interactions and speaking and listening practice.

In a position statement, the National Council of Teachers of English (NCTE, 2014) suggests that, "In the area of student engagement, findings consistently show the value of small classes" (para. 7). Yes, it can be intimidating at times to think about engaging this many 13-year-olds at once and getting them to buy into our why of the day. However, do not underestimate the power of collaboration and co-teaching! We can turn a simple read-aloud into a live representation of what a parallel reading structure may look like. We can model book club discussions, turn and talks, talking to the text, and so much more to instantly grab students' attention. We can transform our classroom into a one-room schoolhouse to kick off our historical fiction unit by immersing students in a particular time period. We can show these new teenagers how to be silly as we model brain breaks to get up and move. We can prepare engaging hooks for our lessons in the forms of snowball fights, concept attainment, music, videos, and so on. Can you do this all by yourself? Absolutely! But as two teachers, we can constantly guide different groups, sit by students who

Video: Combined Brain Break

> **"NO ONE CARES HOW MUCH YOU KNOW UNTIL THEY KNOW HOW MUCH YOU CARE."**
> **- Theodore Roosevelt**

need more support, or join a discussion group to get them going.

Matthew Lynch (2017) continues, "Not surprisingly, students describe themselves as having better relationships with their teachers in smaller classes and evaluate both these classes and their teachers more positively than do their peers in larger classes" (para. 7). While this may be true of large classes with a single teacher, our collaborative relationship and co-teaching have maintained the more positive student-teacher relationships found in small classes with single teachers. How do we know? We have our students rate us. We survey them throughout the year and maintain dialogue journals with them to give them the opportunity to easily and privately share their thoughts and feelings about how class is going. The feedback we've received from the dialogue journals has been nothing but positive. Students love the combined classroom and the opportunities to interact with more of their peers. A lot of the feedback we've received concerns our delivery of co-taught instruction and our way of teaching. Students have generally felt heard and cared for in our class and looked forward to ELA, even if it's not their favorite subject.

Pushing the Boundaries on Social-Emotional Learning

This past year, we have been immersed in researching and implementing social-emotional learning (SEL) strategies within our classroom. Our collaborative professional practice goal was to initiate and maintain regular "Circle Ups," a restorative justice practice, as a way to build classroom community and develop problem-solving skills within our students.

While 56-plus students in one classroom is not typically considered ideal, we argue that with established routines, expectations, and purposeful collaboration, stress levels and behavioral problems are the same as if we only had 25 students in our class at a time. When we say "Circle Up!" to our class, students understand exactly what they need to do, and they find their place in a giant circle around our classroom. We use this strategy to build the climate and culture of our combined class, and it has given our classroom a sense of community and belonging. Every student has opportunities to have their voice heard, from answering a fun question to offering ideas on how to improve our classroom routine. As stated by Brad Weinstein (2019), co-author of Hacking

School Discipline, in one of his blog posts, "If students feel like they are valued, they are less likely to act out and more likely to maintain a positive environment" (para. 1).

We are proud to say that our students hear, comprehend, utilize, and evaluate their use of SEL vocabulary daily. To get to this level of understanding, we developed a rubric centered around the five SEL competencies: responsible decision making, relationship skills, social awareness, self-awareness, and self-management (CASEL, 2021). We set a classroom goal of where we think we should be at different times in the school year, and then students reflect and evaluate their daily behavior and performance in these different areas.

Videos:
Transition to Circle Up | Combined Circle Up

DRAMA Rubric: How are we integrating the SEL competencies as a class

	1	2	3	4	5
Decision Making	*Teacher* must step in to manage decision-making; class is very disorganized.	Decisions are *difficult* to reach; class has trouble moving from one task to another. *Arguing* is present.	Decisions were made with *some* struggles and may have *lacked* reflection. Organization is *somewhat* maintained.	Decisions were made by *identifying* the problem, *analyzing* situations, *evaluating*, and *reflecting*. Organization is maintained.	Decisions were made quickly based on **ethical standards, safety concerns,** and **social norms**. Class moved *directly* from one task to another.
Relationship Skills	Positive communication and social skills were *not* used to interact with others. Active listening was *not* present in partners or groups.	Positive communication and social skills were used *infrequently* to interact with others. Active listening was present in *few* partners or groups.	Positive communication and social skills were used *some* of the time to interact with others. Active listening was present in *some* partners or groups.	Positive communication and social skills were used *most* of the time to interact with others. Active listening was present in *most* partners or groups.	**Positive** communication and social skills were used with others. **Active listening** was present in *all* partners or groups.
Self-**A**wareness	Students *struggled* to understand how their emotions influence behavior. *Few or no* students were focused and there were *many* disruptions.	Students *struggled* to understand how their emotions influence behavior. *Some* students were focused, but distractions were *present* and *disruptive*.	*Some* students were aware of their emotions, thoughts, and values, and how they influence behavior. Students were *somewhat* focused/on task.	*Most* students were aware of their emotions, thoughts, and values, and how they influence behavior. *Almost all* students were focused/on task.	*Everyone* was aware of their **emotions, thoughts,** and **values**. *All* students were **focused/on task**.
Self-**M**anagement	Students may or may not set goals. A growth mindset is *not* present.	Students set goals. *Few* students exhibit a growth mindset.	Students set goals. *Some* students exhibit a growth mindset.	Students set, monitor, and *often* adapt goals. Growth mindset is present in *MOST* students.	Students set, monitor, adapt, and evaluate goals to achieve success. **Growth mindset** is present in *ALL* students.
Social **A**wareness	Empathy is *lacking* and/or students do not yet understand what that means or how it looks. Students *do not* show respect to individuals in our classroom.	*Few* students display empathy and are still learning what that means and how it looks. Respect is shown *inconsistently* and/or to *few* individuals in our classroom.	*Some* students display empathy in interactions and discussions while others are still learning what that looks like. Respect is shown, but may be *inconsistent*.	*Most* students demonstrate an empathetic mindset. *Most* individuals in our classroom are respectful in interactions with others.	**Empathy** is at the center of *ALL* interactions and classroom discussions. **Respect** is shown to *ALL* individuals in our classroom.

We stress to students that while learning the content is important, our goal for each and every one of them is to become a kind and truly decent human being. Collaboration is essential in this goal, considering the best way to learn empathy and kindness is to see them modeled before you. As co-teachers, we are always cognizant of how we treat each other and speak to each other. Part of setting the expectation is showing students how to speak, respond, and interact with their peers.

Pushing the Boundaries on Differentiation of Instruction

As teachers, we hear this word all the time: differentiation! And there are many questions to consider with regards to it:

- How are you meeting the needs of all your learners?
- How are you providing enrichment opportunities?
- What about the students who are below grade level?

Having a shared classroom with as many students as we have, differentiation looks different within our walls.

When we look at differentiating instruction with a large number of students, it is easy to believe that some must get overlooked. However, there's also a great deal of potential in a situation like ours. For example, students are almost always able to partner with others who are working at a similar reading/writing level, simply because having more students creates more options for grouping and pairing. We work diligently to make sure that students

are joined with other classmates who are compatible, have similar interests, and are working in complementary ways to meet identified benchmarks. In our class we teachers select a reading/writing partner for each student based on data, along with reading and writing behaviors. During mini-lessons, students sit with their partners and subsequently transition into partner practice. We have found that, despite the large class, students feel comfortable even in the large group setting during the mini-lesson because of the consistency of their reading/writing partner. They build a strong relationship with that classmate and become better able to understand how they learn. Especially when students are first applying something new, we have found great success with student partnerships.

Flexible grouping is another key component in effective differentiation. We often use this strategy after our mini-lesson and during independent work time. Our flexible groups change weekly based on several factors. We may use data from a pre-assessment to determine groups for a certain skill or standardized test data to form strategy groups. Other times, we'll create random groupings to introduce a new concept or factor in student choice to increase engagement. Carol Ann Tomlinson and Tonya R. Moon (2014) describe flexible grouping as follows: "Flexible grouping stresses the importance of proactive instructional planning to ensure that students regularly and frequently have the opportunity to work with a wide variety of peers" (p. 12). To streamline our collaboration and planning for different groups, we tend to keep students with peers who are working at similar reading and writing levels together to better differentiate essential skills. With our large class size, however, students are still working with a variety of peers, even in our leveled groupings. Regardless of how we group for any given week, we want diverse and varied opportunities for our learners. We also want to avoid students feeling stuck in a less challenging group or elevated in the "smart" group.

Pushing the Boundaries on Conferring With Students

In 2012, John Hattie reported that teachers do the talking 70 to 80 percent of the time or more (as cited in Shrum, 2019). It is true—teachers love to talk. Although we know that the more students are engaged in academic conversations, the more they are learning, letting students do the talking is not as easy as it sounds. Conferring with individual students is nothing new. Yet, we have found that conferring with a small student group decreases the amount of teacher talk and increases the amount of time students have to speak.

In spite of the challenge, we do confer individually with students as well. Our teacher-student conferences follow a set structure: begin with a compliment, observe the student to understand how to grow the reader/writer, and offer teaching points and links to future reading/writing that the student will do. Many teachers would agree that one-on-one conferring provides students with the most accurate data of what they can do and allows for the best instruction because it reveals

what each student needs at that time, at their current level of reading/writing. It also helps build relationships between the teacher and the student to the point where students feel more comfortable opening up in a one-to-one setting. We have found conferring with students to be most beneficial. In fact, we find conferring to be one of the most important instruction activities we do all day! However, we challenge the belief that conferring can only be done one-on-one.

Another way we confer is with a small group of students who need work in a common skill. While each strategy or small group conference may look a little different, the essential components remain the same: research, link, compliment, teaching point, teacher model, student application. These components do not just come from the teacher. Instead, the students jump in to share a strategy or when they notice something they can compliment one another on. Students can also see several student examples and apply what they see to their own work right away. We enjoy this form of conferring because it builds students' confidence by being vulnerable together. Here are some questions we often consider:

- Am I going to reinforce the mini-lesson because something isn't sinking in?

- Am I going to present a challenge by introducing a new skill?

- Should I explicitly model the same strategy with a different text?

Regardless of topic, our group conference ends with a share out about how students will incorporate the new skill into their individual work as they continue to complete the task independently.

This small group conferring model certainly decreases teacher talk and increases students' opportunities to practice their oral language skills. Students are complimenting each other, sharing what they notice, and identifying their goals for future application of skills. We cannot forget the benefit of conferring and relationship building. Not only are students building stronger relationships with the teacher, but they are forming stronger bonds with each other as they become more invested in their learning together.

STUDENT SUCCESS STORIES

Just like any classroom, students learn and master skills at their own pace. We are confident that students will be successful academically, socially, and emotionally in our classroom environment. A few students and their special circumstances stand out to us when we think of our variety of success stories.

Success with English Language Development

Rodrigo is a 13-year-old English learner who has struggled behaviorally and academically in the past. He came into seventh grade with an English proficiency level of "Expanding," according to WIDA. He has also been in our Tier II reading group for interventions during our building-wide intervention time. This year, Rodrigo has consistently increased his STAR reading scores. As we've shared the data with him and provided motivation and encouragement, this student's attitude and mindset have changed drastically. He comes to class with a positive attitude, puts forth his best effort, and participates more and more. Figure 13 shows Rodrigo's growth over three months on the STAR reading assessments.

He has been steadily improving, and his confidence has been growing. Not only have Rodrigo's academics improved tremendously, but we have also seen limited behavior referrals. This is an extraordinary improvement from the past two years. So far this year, he has only had

19-20	Fall	7	Greenville Middle School	9/10/2019	4.7	567	5.0	21	Intervention	Basic	775L	775	33.0	Intervention
19-20	ProgMon	7	Greenville Middle School	11/18/2019	5.0	616	5.4	25	On Watch	Basic	850L	850	35.8	On Watch
19-20	ProgMon	7	Greenville Middle School	12/3/2019	5.3	640	5.6	27	On Watch	Basic	885L	885	37.1	On Watch

Figure 13

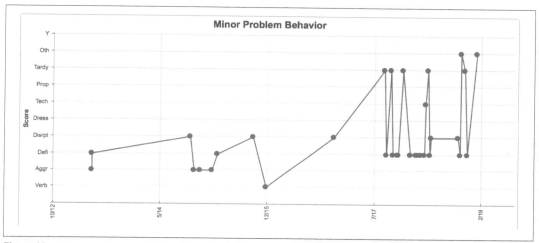

Figure 14

one behavior referral, and that was from an incident on the bus before school. As you can see in Figure 14, all negative behavioral data refers to previous years.

We strongly believe a huge part of Rodrigo's success is due to our collaboration and planning. Both of us have ESL certifications and experience teaching English learners. It doesn't matter who is working one-on-one with this student or any student; we both understand best practices and how to differentiate for Rodrigo. Since we have been heavily focused on Tier II students, when we plan for our guided reading groups, we consider offering a wealth of background knowledge in the form of pictures, stories, videos, and vocabulary development. We work with the same group for a week and then switch the groups between us. It has been extremely helpful for one of us to work intensely with Rodrigo's group and then share our notes and progress so the other teacher can provide a different, purposeful focus the following week.

Success with Emotional Behavioral Disability

Thomas is a 13-year-old with an emotional-behavioral disability. Last year, this student received a pull-out reading intervention for 20 minutes daily. He also utilized the special education resource room frequently. Due to the large amount of class time he missed, however, he fell behind academically, and his negative behaviors increased when he took part in the general classroom.

So far this school year, Thomas has remained in our ELA class for its entirety every day. The special education teacher who is with us during Thomas's ELA block has mentioned how impressed he is with both Thomas's behavior and his participation in content-related discussions. When asked why he has shown success, this teacher credits the classroom climate we have established and the utilization of different teaching techniques.

This student's former teachers explained that he was not in the regular education classroom much last year, and when he was present, he exhibited extremely distracting behaviors. This year in our ELA class, Thomas is excited to participate and contribute to whole-class discussions. Being able to collaborate and plan out our different roles on a given day is extremely important to Thomas's success. We keep in check his particular behaviors that are often distracting, and we place one of us next to him during a lesson or schedule one of us to check in with him at different times throughout our ELA block. We also put him in strategy groups with one of the teachers in the room, including the special education teacher, so that he is with a teacher or near an adult as often as possible.

Success with Supporting Positive Student Outcomes

Oliver is a 13-year-old boy whose actions are sometimes challenging. On occasion, he leaves the classroom without permission, exhibits physical aggression toward other students, and refuses to work. We noticed some of this behavior at the beginning of the school year, as reading and writing were somewhat of a trigger. Our colleagues also shared similar experiences and concerns with Oliver.

It wasn't long before we began noticing positive changes in Oliver, and we believe our classroom environment played a big factor in this transition. Oliver was used to being closely watched by adults, and we found success when giving him increased freedom in the classroom setting. In our class, this student had more choice in seating options and reading material. We also noticed that his behavior changed for the better once we mixed up our combined class seating, creating additional options for student combinations.

One of the biggest successes we saw in him is the growth displayed during our Station Teaching, especially in our teacher-guided groups. We noticed Oliver's increased participation and focus, as well as a more positive attitude. With careful planning and purposeful grouping with this specific student in mind, his confidence grew, and a trusting relationship began.

Another factor that contributed to our success with Oliver was that there were two of us to help build positive relationships. If one of us tried to redirect and noticed escalated behaviors, the other would approach him after a few minutes using a different technique. If the same person was continuously redirecting, we would see explosive behavior like the other teachers on our team. By the end of the school year, Oliver's academic progress was assessed as "at mastery" or "exceeds" in all of the essential standards.

●●● CONCLUSION

In this chapter, we have discussed the co-planning, co-teaching, co-assessment, and co-reflection components of teacher collaboration for the co-taught classroom and how these components specifically apply to our unique partnership. We have learned the importance of acclimating to each other's personalities and teaching styles and capitalizing on each other's strengths to become one classroom community. This pedagogy that we have developed improves and strengthens our instruction. We have provided relevant research on best co-teaching practices, as well as insight into how we are pushing the boundaries of those practices with our combined classroom. We know that we will continue to be challenged regarding our unique situation, but we are confident in our approach. Our constant collaboration, even in a super-sized classroom, is what's best for our kids.

References and Further Resources

Collaborative for Academic, Social, and Emotional Learning (CASEL). (2021). https://casel.org/

Dove, M. G., & Honigsfeld, A. (2018). *Co-teaching for English learners: A guide to collaborative planning, instruction, assessment, and reflection.* Corwin.

DuFour, R., DuFour, R., Eaker, R., Many, T. W., & Mattos, M. (2006). *Learning by doing: A handbook for professional learning communities at work.* Solution Tree.

Hanover Research. (2012). *The effectiveness of the co-teaching model: Literature review.* https://www.ousd.org/cms/lib/CA01001176/Centricity/Shared/The%20Effectiveness%20of%20the%20Co-Teaching%20Model-Inclusion%20Material.pdf

Irwin, R. (2007). Culture shock: Negotiating feelings in the field. *Anthropology Matters, 9*(1). https://doi.org/10.22582/am.v9i1.64

Lynch, M. (2017). *Does class size really matter?* The Edvocate. www.theedadvocate.org/class-size-really-matter/

National Council of Teachers of English (NCTE). (2014). *Why class size matters today.* https://ncte.org/statement/why-class-size-matters

Shrum, D. L. (2019). Empower students through individual conferences. *ASCD.* https://www.ascd.org/el/articles/empower-students-through-individual-conferences

Solution Tree. (2021). *All things PLC, all in one place.* www.allthingsplc.info/

Tomlinson, C. A., & Moon, T. R. (2014). *Assessment and student success in a differentiated classroom.* ASCD.

Weinstein, B. (2019). Circle up for a better climate and culture. *BehaviorFlip's Blog.* https://blog.behaviorflip.com/circle-up-for-a-better-climate-and-culture/

3

Building
Teacher Capacity
to Support ELs

CONSULT
COLLABORATE
COACH

Lindsay Manzella and
Jane Russell Valezy

SNAPSHOT

The American International School
of Budapest (AISB) is a private, non-profit international school established by the U.S. Embassy in 1973. AISB offers an international curriculum from Pre-K (3-year-olds) to grade 12 and currently has just over 900 students representing 60 different nationalities. Of these, 240 students are in middle school, 30 percent of whom are English learners (ELs) receiving English as an Additional Language (EAL)[1] support. Additionally, about 75 percent of the overall student population does not speak English as a first language.

We are two EAL teachers out of a team of three in the middle school, and we are each assigned to one grade level: Lindsay supports seventh grade, and Jane supports eighth grade. We teach in a hybrid model: students up to WIDA language proficiency level 5 attend an EAL class three times per six-day cycle in lieu of a world language class. We also provide support for teachers and students in the form of co-planning, co-teaching, co-assessing, and, more recently, coaching. We both completed a two-year literacy coaching certification program, and we are exploring how to coach teachers in building their capacity for providing effective language support—not only for ELs, but for all students.

[1] EAL (English as an Additional Language) is used in our context because many of our students are learning English not as a second language, but as a third, fourth, or even fifth language. They may already be bilingual in other languages and are adding on English in addition. It also honors and emphasizes the idea of "additive bi-/multilingualism" in which they are not replacing their other languages but adding another one.

SETTING THE STAGE

At our school, we have been using a collaborative model to support the English language development of our students for several years. This model has helped us raise the focus on supporting ELs in their academic language development by integrating language support into academic learning. As our EL student numbers grew, we were able to designate one full-time EAL teacher per grade level, allowing us to immerse ourselves in the academic content for that grade and attend to the academic language that all students needed to learn. However, we struggled for time. We could not engage with all of our ELs long enough for this integrated support to be meaningful. They needed support all day long, not just when EAL teachers were in their content classrooms. Additionally, we were still spread too thin as we were each trying to divide our time between multiple class sections per subject, collaborating and co-teaching with several different teachers and teaching stand-alone EAL classes. Our students received this integrated support for one period per day, but what about the rest of the day? They were struggling, and teachers were struggling.

We began to consider ways to have a greater impact on student learning. As a result, we embarked on a new approach to EAL support, shifting our focus toward building teacher capacity. We believe that assisting content teachers in developing their skills to instruct ELs can have a greater effect on student learning since these teachers have more direct contact with students themselves. After several

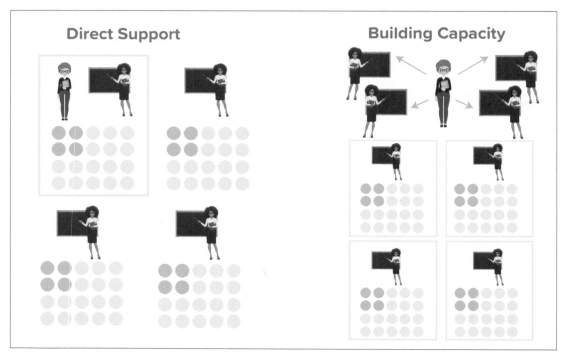

Direct Support · Building Capacity

Used with permission of the authors.

years of trying various ways of building teacher capacity through professional development efforts, we participated in a training about instructional coaching and learned about the superior benefits coaching brings to student learning. Because coaching is embedded professional development that is responsive to the individual needs of the teacher and the students in the moment, it leads to greater uptake and application of teacher learning (Aguilar, 2013). We wanted to apply a coaching model to our work in supporting English learners.

How is what we do in a coaching model different from collaborating as we were before? One of the biggest shifts is the way we approach working with teachers. We had always helped teachers plan supports for ELs in their classes. However, now our focus is less on scaffolding and supporting students directly during content lessons and more on facilitating the content teachers' ability to provide language support and incorporate scaffolding and other strategies for students in their classes. We do this by using open-ended questioning to guide teachers to assess for themselves what students' needs are and to facilitate brainstorming ideas for support that can be built into the class instruction, with or without an EAL teacher in the room. The content teacher has ownership over the support, and the support is designed to be in place in all of their classes, even when the EAL teacher is not present. In this way, the strategies carry over into the content teachers' instructional practices in all of their classes. By working with each content teacher to build their capacity to

embed support for ELs into instructional practices, we are able to reach all of the ELs that each teacher works with throughout the day. Our role as EAL teachers has subtly shifted to become more about being facilitators than always the direct sources of student support.

In addition to building teacher capacity, we continue to give suggestions and share our resources and ideas for supporting ELs. We are still the EAL specialists and bring that lens to our co-planning sessions. However, to have the greatest impact on student learning, we have begun to look at how we can not only support student needs but the needs of teachers as well. We do this by working with teachers along a continuum of Consult—Collaborate—Coach (Lipton & Wellman, 2017). The consulting and collaborating is closer to the work we had previously done in directly supporting students. The coaching, however, focuses more on building the capacity of teachers to take ownership of student support.

When we **consult**, we take on the role of the language support expert, either providing materials and resources when asked or directly suggesting how to support students. For example, a content teacher might come to us a day before the lesson and ask for a strategy to support ELs with a difficult reading passage. We might then provide the content-area teacher with two strategies to choose from.

When we **collaborate**, we work alongside content teachers to co-plan lessons with specific student support, then decide what

> By shifting our focus to empowering and building capacity in content teachers to take ownership and adopt language support strategies in their regular teaching practices, we can use our time more flexibly to support students and teachers where it is most needed.

that support will look like in the classroom, including whether the lesson will be co-taught and how. This might take the form of planning an upcoming unit with the content teacher, looking at the unit standards, and developing some language objectives to support their goals for the students. We may decide to co-teach a lesson to the whole class or each teach a specific strategy to the group. Finally, we might co-assess the student work and reflect on the process.

When we **coach,** we use specific strategies to support the content-area teacher's thinking, problem-solving, goal determination, and reflection in supporting ELs. This work is student-focused ("What do the students need to be successful?") rather than teacher-focused ("How can the teacher improve his or her practice?"). It may involve working with a particular content teacher for a finite amount of time (a few weeks or a unit) and cycling around different teachers over the school year rather than co-teaching continuously with the same content teachers. In coaching, our role is not to determine the goals for the students

but rather to support the content-area teachers in coming up with their own goals for student learning. Once a goal is set, we can collaboratively identify strategies to help students meet that goal. We then support the content-area teacher in implementing these strategies by using various coaching techniques (modeling, co-teaching, guided reflection, etc.).

This is what it might look like if a language arts teacher getting ready to start a unit on poetry decides to work with us in a coaching cycle: We would begin with a planning meeting where we take on a coaching role and use a structured, open-ended questioning strategy to guide the language arts teacher in determining a goal for students based on their needs. Then we would work together for the duration of the unit using a continuous cycle of co-planning, co-teaching or in-class coaching, and co-reflection. At the end of the unit, we would reflect on the entire process together, and then the EAL teacher would move on to start a new coaching cycle with, for example, the science teacher.

We aim to be flexible when working with teachers, moving along the Consult—Collaborate—Coach continuum fluidly as needed. Consulting, collaborating, and coaching are all important aspects of our collaborative practice with teachers. Where we fall on the continuum at any given moment depends on who we are working with, the unit being planned, the amount of time available, and so on.

We have been able to make the coaching model work for us, particularly the use of coaching cycles, by radically changing the way we structure our time as EAL teachers. While previously we thought of our time in terms of direct student contact (making sure each student had an equitable number of minutes with the EAL teacher), we now think of our time in terms of supporting teachers to meet student needs whether or not we are scheduled to be in the classroom. In the past, we could never seem to be enough for our students; it's impossible to be everywhere at once. By shifting our focus to empowering and building capacity in content teachers to take ownership and adopt language support strategies in their regular teaching practices, we can use our time more flexibly to support students and teachers where it is most needed. Meanwhile, we know that students are getting what they need from the content-area teachers who are with them the most. So, while our student support is now more indirect at times, it is also more powerful because it has a wider impact.

BLUEPRINT

We have been fortunate enough to have administrative support in shaping our coaching model approach. The following actions have been key in helping shift the approach to language support in our middle school.

Focus on Building Teacher Capacity to Have More Impact on Student Learning

With the rising population of ELs in our schools, content teachers need to be prepared to meet the needs of these students in their classrooms. EAL teachers cannot be everywhere at once, so we must empower content teachers to support language learners. By building capacity in content teachers, we can reach more students than in either traditional support models or co-teaching models and thus have more impact on student learning.

Use a Coaching Model to Work With Teachers

A coaching model follows a structure of co-planning, co-teaching, and co-reflecting to build teacher capacity. The EAL coach facilitates teacher goal-setting through strategic questioning, but teachers choose the goals for the collaborative work. Within the coaching model, the EAL teacher does not always need to take on the role of a coach. The EAL teacher can and should move along the continuum of Consult—Collaborate—Coach as fits the teacher's situation or needs.

Maintain a Flexible Schedule to Support Students

Flexibility in our schedules allows us to work with teachers in "support cycles," spending our time where it is most needed in ways that have the greatest impact on the greatest number of students. Our collaboration may look different from teacher to teacher at any given time. For example, an EAL teacher might be involved in a coaching cycle with one teacher, regularly co-teaching with another, and collaboratively planning with another two teachers as needed. Flexibility is the key to giving teachers what they need to support students.

Keep Student Needs at the Forefront When Working With Teachers

Coaching should be student-centered, with learning goals as the driving force (as opposed to coaching that "fixes" teachers' instructional practices). Student learning targets and student work remain the focus at all times. Coaching conversations are strategically structured to keep the focus on student needs. Notice that in the Conversation Templates on pg. 63, the questions frame conversations around goals for student learning and what supports might help them achieve those goals, rather than focusing on the teacher's instructional practice.

Approach Collaboration With the Mindset that the EAL Teacher and Content Teacher Are Equal Partners Supporting Students

As in any collaborative or co-teaching relationship, in order for the partnership to work and be positive for everyone involved (including students), both collaborating teachers must enter the relationship as equally valued partners who bring their own strengths to the table.

Collaborate to Support the Academic Language Development of All Learners, Not Just ELs

No one is a native speaker of academic language (Maxwell, 2013); therefore, all students must learn and have the opportunity to practice academic English. When working with teachers to plan language support, arrange ways to build in support for all students. Before we used a coaching model, our support targeted and benefited only the ELs we worked with directly. Now all students can benefit from the built-in language support. The teachers we work with also say this is one of their biggest takeaways.

Work With Administration to Establish a Schoolwide Culture of Collaboration and Coaching

Administrative support is essential to upholding all of these principles as schoolwide beliefs. Administrators must be willing to be flexible in scheduling and assigning teachers' contact hours, understanding that teacher-to-teacher contact time is key. This time is even more important than the EAL teacher's student contact time. Administrators also lead the way in modeling the equal value of each teacher partner and the value of supporting the academic language development of all learners.

HIGH IMPACT STRATEGIES

The following strategies and tools, which we have adapted from the coaching realm, have been indispensable in coaching teachers to strengthen the language support they provide and impact student learning.

Consult—Collaborate—Coach

In the continuum of Consult—Collaborate—Coach, we as EAL teachers move fluidly as needed between:

- providing the EAL lens and making suggestions (consulting),
- co-planning and co-teaching with content teachers (collaborating), and
- guiding teachers to set goals, try new strategies for integrating language support in their instruction, and reflect on the teaching and learning in their classes (coaching).

Within a coaching cycle, or even a single planning meeting, we may shift between consulting, collaborating, and coaching as appropriate.

	WHAT IS IT?	WHAT DOES IT LOOK LIKE?	WHEN IS IT USED?
Consult	The EAL teacher serves as an expert, providing resources and information.	• Offering information • Providing problem analysis and perspective • Proposing ideas and solutions • Finding and sharing resources • Providing information about language learning and acquisition	• When the content teacher does not have familiarity with or knowledge of a particular strategy • When the content teacher asks for resources or strategies
Collaborate	The EAL teacher works alongside the content-area teacher to develop ideas and strategies. The EAL teacher and content teacher co-teach the lessons and co-assess the outcomes.	• Co-generating ideas, lessons, and supports • Co-analyzing problems and solutions • Co-developing success criteria • Co-assessing student outcomes	• During most planning meetings • When looking at student work • When creating rubrics
Coach	The EAL teacher facilitates and supports the content-area teacher's thinking through open-ended questioning to set student-focused goals, plan appropriate instructional strategies, and later reflect on the process. The EAL teacher co-teaches and models strategies.	• Asking open-ended questions • Facilitating teacher idea production • Enhancing teacher capacities for reflection, planning, and problem-solving around language support • Co-teaching • Modeling	• At the beginning and end of a unit, assignment, or series of lessons to facilitate planning and reflecting • To develop lasting, embedded instructional practices that support ELs

Conversation Templates for Planning and Reflecting

Conversation templates provide a structure to help us guide teachers in a) setting goals for student learning during the planning phase and then b) considering student outcomes in the reflection phase. Using open-ended questioning during planning and reflection meetings helps support teachers in thinking about how to integrate language support into their teaching practices. By guiding teachers to choose their own goals and teaching strategies (rather than having teachers rely on us to tell them how to provide support), we can ensure teachers have ownership over the instruction, assistance, and guidance they provide to students.

Using the **Conversation Template for Planning,** we guide the teacher in setting student-centered goals based on both the learning standards and the assessment of student needs. In a planning meeting, the questioning structure focuses on learning targets:

- Goal-setting
- Identifying success indicators
- Planning supports
- Reflecting on the effectiveness of the process

Conversation Template for Planning

Establish Context:
Tell me a bit about the unit students are working on (data: standards, unit planner).

What is the lesson we are focusing on? How do you envision that lesson/class period?

Set Goal:
What is the goal of this lesson? What do you want students to understand or be able to do by the end of this lesson? Where are they now?

Determine Success Indicators:
How will you know students are successful? What evidence do you want to collect? (Use this information to determine next steps).

Plan Instruction:
What instructional practices will help students reach the goal? What strategies have you used before that might work well here?

Set Practice Focus:
What do you want to do well while teaching this lesson? How might you know you are doing it?

Plan Logistics:
What specific task will we each be responsible for during planning and instruction?

Reflect on Coaching Conversation:
What are some ways this conversation/collaboration has helped plan for the lesson/unit?

Conversation Template for Reflection

Overall Impressions:

How do you feel the lesson went?

Causal Factors:

What do you think most affected that outcome? What factors do you think led to the success/difficulties you identified?

Looking Forward:

What learning do you plan to take forward? What did you learn that you plan to use to guide future lessons?

Next Steps:

What will your next steps be?

Reflect on the Coaching Process:

What are some ways this coaching process has been helpful for you and your students?

Used with permission of the authors.

Using the **Conversation Template for Reflection,** we guide teachers in assessing the effectiveness of chosen strategies and making decisions for the next steps. Each teacher can decide whether to continue with the same goal or move on to a new one. Teachers also reflect on their personal learning about their teaching practice and how to apply that to future lessons.

In both conversation templates, it is important to use open-ended, probing questions rather than closed or leading questions. Instead of "How about giving students a reading guide for this text?" we would ask, "Where do you see students encountering difficulties with this text?" or "What kind of support strategies might work to help students understand this text?" This strategic, open-ended questioning is a crucial component of our coaching work with teachers. As one of the math teachers we work with commented, the structured questions prompt teachers to think about the dynamics of the lesson and reflect in ways that are hard to do alone.

Instructional Playbook

Our instructional playbook is a tool created by our EAL team to support building teacher capacity in strategies for ELs. Inspired by Jim Knight's 2018 book, *The Impact Cycle*, it is a curated collection of high impact strategies from our own repertoire that are known to be greatly beneficial for students. Knight recommends that coaches create their own playbooks using the strategies they know and use. Each strategy in our team's playbook is described in a one-page format, with a concise description and easy-to-follow checklist. The playbook is a resource for us to share strategies while collaborating with content teachers; whether during planning meetings, while modeling strategies in class, or as needed in a lesson. By sharing and using these strategies with teachers in the classroom, we are building capacity in the content-area teacher to support ELs.

SAMPLE
Strategy: Vocabulary Predictions

In One Sentence:
This strategy gives students the opportunity to switch on to the content of the text and build vocabulary and background knowledge in the process.

How It Works:
Before reading, students are given time to consider what they already know about a topic and generate content-area vocabulary they might expect to come up in the text. Students then explain their reasons for choosing each vocabulary word. Through sharing their list of content-related vocabulary and backing up their choices with explanations of how each one connects to the topic, the class builds up a collective knowledge of the vocabulary and conceptual understanding related to the content.

Checklist:

What to do	✓
Before reading, tell students what the topic of the text is.	
Ask students what they already know about this topic, and make a visible list of ideas generated.	
Ask students what vocabulary words they might expect to find in a text about this topic, and make a visible list.	
As students generate words, ask them to explain why they might expect to read that word in a text on this topic.	
Give students time to note any vocabulary that is new to them and what it seems to mean based on the explanation given by their classmates.	
After reading, follow up by going back to the class vocabulary list and having students identify which words were indeed in the text.	
Finish by giving students time to go back to their own lists of new vocabulary to add to or revise their definitions as needed, based on what they read or learned about that word.	

STUDENT (AND TEACHER) SUCCESS STORIES

In their third year working together, grade 7 EAL teacher Lindsay switched to a coaching model to collaborate with grade 7 science teacher Darrick. Notice how Lindsay's role in the partnership shifts fluidly along the continuum of Consult—Collaborate—Coach throughout their work on the unit. Lindsay describes their process:

Darrick and I started the semester with a coaching conversation to set a goal for student learning. Before adopting a coaching model, I would often give suggestions in our planning meetings about what support ELs might need or how to highlight language in science class. This year, rather than give advice and ideas, I used the Conversation Template for Reflection to allow Darrick to decide on a goal for all students that he felt could really make a difference. From there, we would be able to collaborate to come up with support and strategies.

Using the method proposed by Jim Knight (2018), I began the coaching cycle by videoing one of Darrick's science lessons to get a "clear picture of reality" in order to set a meaningful goal for student learning (rather than teacher practice). We both viewed the video, and then I facilitated a reflection conversation with Darrick to talk about the lesson and decide on a goal for student learning. From the video, Darrick noted two aspects of the lesson that he might want to focus on for possible goals: building science vocabulary and developing academic conversations. I asked Darrick which of the two had the potential to make the biggest impact on his students, and he decided on academic conversations, noting that "it's more robust and there are more ways to use it."

Rather than give Darrick ideas for how to teach students to have academic conversations as I would have in the past, I asked him to describe what it would look like for students to have a meaningful academic conversation. Darrick explained that the students would work together to solidify their understanding of the topic.

Video: Coaching Conversation #1 with Darrick

They would use conversation skills such as paraphrasing and questioning without sounding as if they were reading directly from the given sentence starters. I then guided the conversation toward setting a specific goal for students concerning conversation skills and success indicators so that we would know that the students had met the goal. Darrick noted that the ultimate goal of student talk is for the students to learn from each other and develop their own thinking, so the success indicators would relate whether the students thought their partner conversations "added to their knowledge" or "changed their thinking," or if their "thinking stayed the same." The measurable goal would be for 90 percent of students to indicate that they "added to their knowledge" or "changed their thinking" on their exit ticket after the conversation. With the specific student-centered goal and success indicators determined, Darrick and I set a time to talk again to plan instruction for meeting the set goal.

At this stage, I shifted along the Consult—Collaborate—Coach continuum from a coaching role to a collaborative one. In our next planning meeting, Darrick and I worked together to design the exit ticket we would use to determine if students had met their goals. Together we decided how the lesson would go and who would teach which parts. Because I was more comfortable teaching academic conversations, I would teach that portion of the lesson. My flexible schedule allowed me to teach the lesson in Darrick's first science class of the day to model the strategy, and then he would repeat the lesson on his own during the other three class sections.

In our next collaborative meeting, I again assumed a coaching approach as Darrick and I sat down to sort the exit tickets from each section to see if the students had met the goal. Together we noticed that most of the students had developed their thinking through partner conversations, but a handful of students in each class didn't think they had benefited from talking with their partner (so about 70 percent in each class met the stated goal). Darrick and I discussed the possible reasons these students didn't indicate that the conversation had helped develop their thinking. Was the conversation off topic? Was it just their perception? Was the outcome the result of ineffective partnerships?

Both Darrick and I agreed that we had made some good progress, but there was more we could do to help students meet the goal we had set. Together we brainstormed some ideas to approach academic conversations in a different way. I looked at my notes and reminded Darrick of some of the ideas he had previously suggested before sharing a few more that I had. We talked through how some of these might look in class and how we could incorporate them into various parts of the unit. Rather than offer a concrete plan of action, I asked Darrick what he thought the next steps should be.

Video:
Coaching
Conversation #2
with Darrick

Sorting student Exit Tickets
in grade 7 science

For the rest of the unit, Darrick and I collaborated on incorporating academic conversation skills into the science lessons. Darrick was now familiar with many of the strategies that we had used in this (and previous) units, so he did not hesitate to use them on his own. Occasionally, I would take on a consulting role, such as when I found a new strategy or idea to offer. At the end of the unit, I again took on the role of coach, using the Conversation Template for Reflection to discuss the progress toward the academic conversation goal for students and whether it made sense to continue, revise, or change the goal for the upcoming unit.

Grade 8 EAL teacher Jane collaborates with English language arts teacher Lisa to support students in developing their writing skills. Notice how the collaboration between Lisa and Jane built teacher capacity to support and scaffold students' work in writing, resulting in a clear and lasting impact on student learning, whether or not Jane co-teaches the lessons in the future. Jane shares her collaboration with Lisa as follows:

Students had just completed a writing assignment and Lisa and I were having a collaborative reflection conversation around the students' work. Lisa noticed that when she gave students writing prompts, despite explicitly telling them what parts needed to be included in their analysis paragraphs (topic sentence, three pieces of textual evidence, their analysis of that evidence), ELs were having a particularly difficult time expressing clear, analytical thinking about the texts. Many misinterpreted the task as summarizing. Some attempted to analyze the text, but their ideas were unclear and difficult to follow. Lisa expressed frustration that the ideas we heard them talk about in class were not coming through in their writing in an organized, coherent way.

Through the reflection conversation, it became clear that students were able to verbally express some good analytical thinking about the texts. However, when it came to writing, they struggled to make those same ideas clear. Based on her language arts standards, Lisa set a goal for students to write clear, organized, coherent analysis paragraphs. Lisa and I discussed strategies that would support this goal and decided that some models of what the writing should look like would probably help, along with some sentence and paragraph frames.

For the next writing assignment, I prepared the language frames while Lisa wrote up a model paragraph. We used color coding to show exactly where and how the scaffolding language was used in the model, making clear how they fit together. When Lisa introduced the assignment, she explained more than just the writing prompt and requirements of the paragraph. We then started (and co-taught) a mini-lesson for the whole class on how to put those pieces together into a coherent paragraph, and we demonstrated how students might use the language frames. The resulting pieces of student writing resembled the modeled structure and demonstrated greater clarity and stronger organization. This increased writing proficiency was seen not only in the ELs' work but in all students' writing.

Upon reflection, Lisa commented that she realized she had been telling students the "what" of their analysis writing, but not the "how." She also noted that although we had initially incorporated this scaffold for the benefit of the EAL students in her classes, she saw "how enormously helpful it was for all the writers in the room." Since that time, Lisa has set up all of her writing tasks similarly, with clear models and structure breakdowns, giving stems to help students convey ideas clearly, and color-coding the parts of the writing to demonstrate how they fit together.

Although I am not always in classes with Lisa, she continues to use the mini-lessons and scaffolds we developed during our collaborative conversations. The quality of student writing in Lisa's language arts classes has increased overall and continues to improve as students practice using these scaffolds. Additionally, because she provides the language supports to the whole class, there is no stigma attached to using them. Most students, ELs and fluent English speakers alike, tend to choose to use them to help keep their ideas clear and organized. In fact, students very often choose to color-code their own writing in the same way to help them keep their writing organized and well-structured. It has become a strategy that students have adopted and continue to use throughout the year and even into high school. Also, because this has become part of Lisa's teaching practice every time she sets a

new writing assignment, all of her students in all of her classes, for every year, benefit from this built-in language support.

———————————————

Grade 8 EAL teacher Jane collaborates with science teacher Joel. In this vignette, Joel and Jane were meeting to discuss an upcoming science unit on plant reproduction. Jane and Joel had collaborated and co-taught this unit in one section of Joel's science classes the previous year, with Jane providing supporting resources and modeling teaching strategies to support students' reading comprehension in science. This example illustrates how the Conversation Template for Reflection guided Joel toward deep reflection on the strategies and resources that impacted student learning, resulting in a plan for going forward to maximize student understanding. In addition, this example also demonstrates the lasting positive impact of coaching-style collaboration to build capacity and empower teachers to support students. Notice how the collaboration between Jane and Joel positively affected learning for a wide sphere of students, not only the ELs that she directly co-taught in that one class section. Jane describes their collaboration as follows:

When it came time to plan for the plant reproduction unit, Joel and I began by reflecting on the previous year's work. I used

the Conversation Template for Reflection as a frame to consider how the unit had gone the previous year to determine what support might be needed for the current year. Through the conversation, Joel also reflected on our work from the previous year, commenting that he felt so much more prepared to teach and support students in the unit this year because of the the work we had done together previously. He expressed how the collaboration had enriched the unit and helped him to prepare for supporting students. Here's what he told me:

> Last year, I wanted the kids to learn about pollinators and animal and plant reproductive success, so I found the chapter in our textbook. But through our co-planning conversations, we realized that the text would be way over the heads of many of the students, so what I was wondering then was, "How can I meet the needs of all the students?" At that point, you found the accompanying text on mutualism, and it was a perfect fit because you knew exactly what the standards were that we had been working toward since the beginning of the unit. You were able to not only find the reading but also guide the students through it as well. You taught first for one of the class sections as a model, and I remember I did a lot more listening and observing the first time. Then for the other class sections, I was able to apply the language strategies that you had used with the students.

Joel also recounted how our collaboration had benefited students. He noted that he had seen clear evidence of the positive

effect on student learning because, in the summative assessment, he had noticed that students (ELs and non-ELs) had incorporated the ideas and learning about pollinators and mutualism into their explanations of plant reproduction, even without those details being an explicit part of the assessment prompt, thereby demonstrating a deeper level of understanding than he had even asked for. More importantly, Joel reported that our collaborative work had supported students not only in that particular lesson and unit but throughout the year by modeling how they could read nonfiction science texts. He noticed that many students benefited from that extra guidance with reading the text, as evidenced in their assessments. He also commented that the positive effects had carried over to his current year's students as well because he was now prepared with the supporting resources and strategies he had learned the previous year to teach the unit in the same way again.

At the end of the meeting, Joel expressed such confidence in going forward with the unit in the same way that we decided additional collaboration and support was not necessary. Instead, we would check in at the end of the unit to reflect on its success. Joel was empowered to provide the support his EL students needed, and my time was opened up to work with another teacher for a coaching cycle.

●●● CONCLUSION

We have found that using a coaching model of EAL support is a more effective way to use our time and helps bring a language-support lens to teachers' instructional planning. With this change in mindset and the support of our administration, coaching techniques and tools allow us to build teacher capacity for student language support in a nonthreatening, student-focused way with a greater, lasting impact on instruction and student learning.

●●●

References and Further Resources

Aguilar, E. (2013). *The art of coaching: Effective strategies for school transformation.* Jossey-Bass.

Knight, J. (2018). *The impact cycle: What instructional coaches should do to foster powerful improvements in teaching.* Corwin.

Lipton, L., & Wellman, B. (2017). *Mentoring matters: A practical guide to learning-focused relationships* (3rd ed.). MiraVia.

Maxwell, L. A. (2013, October 28). Common Core ratchets up language demands for English-learners. *Education Week.* https://www.edweek. org/ew/articles/2013/10/30/10cc-academiclanguage. h33.html

Sweeney, D. (2011). *Student-centered coaching: A guide for K-8 coaches and principals.* Corwin.

4

Authentic
Co-Assessments

DESIGNING, TRACKING, AND ANALYZING STUDENT PROGRESS

Jackie Griffin and
Stephanie Just

SNAPSHOT

Kildeer Countryside School District 96 is located in Buffalo Grove, IL. It consists of a kindergarten center, four elementary school buildings, and two middle schools. We work as language development coaches (LDCs) at different elementary schools within the district, both schools having between 25 and 30 percent English learner (EL) populations. To ensure an optimum learning environment, students who qualify for English language support learn alongside English-fluent speakers in general education classes. In this way, all students benefit from the diverse talents and experiences that each student offers. These classes are supported by a language development coach. In total, there are twenty-four LDCs supporting ELs across all seven buildings; each language development coach supports up to five classes.

As LDCs, we work to build the capacity of teachers to make content accessible for language learners and to grow in the four language domains: listening, speaking, reading, and writing. As part of our partnership with classroom teachers, we develop formative assessments for each unit of study that determine students' language development progress within academic targets. These assessments serve as diagnostic data that supports teachers in making informed decisions about instruction so that every child is successful. This continuous review ensures that each child in our system, specifically ELs, receives an equitable education as well as the appropriate support to succeed in both academics and English language development.

SETTING THE STAGE

When teachers continually collect data, collaborate with team members using the data trends, and plan instruction based on the students' needs, students will achieve at higher levels. Our teams of teachers and coaches work to understand the language and academic demands, the pacing of learning targets, and the benchmark assessments of upcoming units. After the team has a shared understanding of the expectations and demands of the unit, they begin creating additional common formative assessments (CFAs) to collect data on students' knowledge and skills throughout the unit. Data from all assessments is used to plan for whole-group, small-group, and individualized instruction. The team collectively selects dates on the calendar to give all assessments, as well as time to collaboratively analyze the data. This process of planning emphasizes that assessments are the first step in the instructional plan, not the final one.

Common formative assessments have proven to be very successful because we unite as a collective team and engage in deep conversations, ensuring all students receive the best instruction possible. After the team administers a CFA, they collaboratively analyze the data. This data analysis allows language coaches to identify how ELs are performing compared to their peers and allows all teachers to see how the whole grade level is achieving. Team members discuss student strengths, areas of growth for students and teachers,

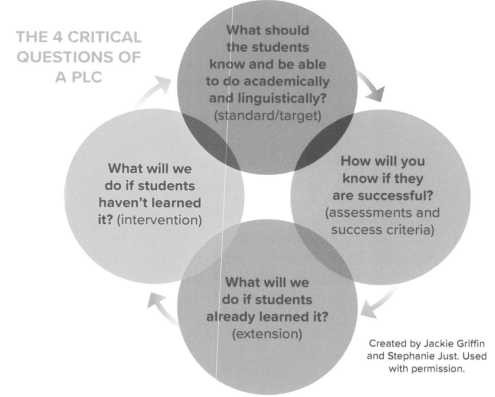

THE 4 CRITICAL QUESTIONS OF A PLC

What should the students know and be able to do academically and linguistically? (standard/target)

How will you know if they are successful? (assessments and success criteria)

What will we do if students already learned it? (extension)

What will we do if students haven't learned it? (intervention)

Created by Jackie Griffin and Stephanie Just. Used with permission.

and the impact of our instructional practices. We determine, as a team, which strategies worked well and what our next steps should be with each group of students. This collective effort supports *all* students—not just the students in one specific class or subgroup. It also creates a safe space for teachers who may feel vulnerable about their data to confer with coaches and teammates who, in turn, can support the next steps. These conversations about assessment empower teachers to meet with small groups of students to deliver purposeful instruction for each and every student based on the data. This continuous process occurs with each CFA. It is based on the four critical questions of a professional learning community (PLC) outlined on p. 74.

We have also explored new ways to unobtrusively assess students daily to gain data that helps guide our instruction. It has truly been a mind shift to go from teaching what the manual says to teaching what the students need. The manual can guide what you are supposed to teach, but ultimately student performance is what tells you what to change in your instruction, who needs more help, and which students are ready to extend their thinking. All of these alterations in instruction are rooted in the data from the assessments. The deep conversations among the team around common formative assessments and the inconspicuous methods used for gathering data have allowed teachers to design unique learning experiences for students that are not scripted from a curriculum handbook but are truly part of an individualized learning plan based on real-time data.

BLUEPRINT

Understand Unit Goals to Create Assessments

To create the most purposeful assessments, we need a strong understanding of each lesson unit. As stated previously, our teams of teachers and coaches engage in powerful conversations before a unit begins to make sure every team member is prepared to teach the unit. We collaborate and analyze to anticipate student needs, embed receptive and expressive language, select appropriate scaffolds, and administer assessments to gather comparable data. To determine if students have met the learning targets, the team develops a collective understanding of those targets, along with the language demands/opportunities and common assessments. Once everyone understands the unit goals, we review previously created common formative assessments and decide which other formal and informal assessments need to be created.

Plan When and How to Incorporate Assessments Throughout the Unit

Once the team has looked through the lessons and decided which assessments are needed, they discuss when and how to include these assessments throughout the unit. We want to ensure consistency among the team members so that all students have an equitable experience when completing assessment tasks.

Questions we consider:

- How will you give instructions?
- How much information can you give the students ahead of time?
- What support can you provide during the assessment?
- How much time can the students have to complete the assignment?
- What will you do if a student doesn't know what to do?

The team discusses all of these questions before the unit begins and again prior to giving the assessments.

Analyze Data and Plan for Future Instruction

After the teachers give a CFA, the team analyzes student work and discusses the trends they notice and possible next steps for students. Figure 1 on page 77 shows an example of the tool we use to capture notes during our collaborative team conversations. Before each conversation, teachers input their student data onto a spreadsheet that is shared with the team of teachers, coaches, and principals. The spreadsheet shows student attainment—extending, mastering, developing, or not mastering—of the learning target. Teachers analyze the student data and identify trends in each class as well as throughout the whole grade level. Next, they discuss each level of mastery. For example, the team talks about the students who received a 1.0, meaning they have

not yet mastered the target. The teachers converse about what specific errors the students made and what instructional strategies will help bring the students to mastery. Then they repeat these conversations for each level of proficiency. At the conclusion of the team session, the teachers commit to trying one of these instructional strategies with a group of students. In addition, the coaches present during these conversations agree to support each teacher in working toward their commitment.

Team conversations continually revolve around student growth, common patterns of student data, celebrations of students' and teachers' successes, and instructional next steps for every level of performance based on shared rubrics. While considering next steps for students to develop, master, and extend the targets, we refer to the strategies and scaffolds the team has previously discussed (see Planning Template Tool, p. 85). As language development coaches, we build the capacity in the team to identify current language levels and the language support needed to advance the skills of our culturally and linguistically diverse students. Having these conversations opens up the door for individualized, differentiated instruction to happen in the classroom. Each group of students may have unique needs—meaning instruction will look different in each classroom—but the goals are the same.

Each group of students may have unique needs—meaning instruction will look different in each classroom—but the goals are the same.

Figure 1: Data conversation tool used in District 96. Used with permission.

1. Celebrate the strengths in the data. Did a particular classroom do extremely well? Find out what happened instructionally in that classroom. Look at samples of student work. What skills did the proficient students demonstrate in their work that set their work apart? Which instructional strategies helped students learn?				
Date Point 1	Data Point 2	Data Point 3	Data Point 4	Data Point 5

2. Reflect on the commitments (#4) from the last data conversation. How did students' growth and understanding of the target change as a result of your instructional plan and teaching?				
	After giving Data Point 2, reflect on the instructional plan your team created. What evidence do you have that your instructional plan was effective?	After giving Data Point 3, reflect on the instructional plan your team created. What evidence do you have that your instructional plan was effective?	After giving Data Point 4, reflect on the instructional plan your team created. What evidence do you have that your instructional plan was effective?	After giving Data Point 5, reflect on the instructional plan your team created. What evidence do you have that your instructional plan was effective?

3. Using your TeacherEase gradebook and samples of student work, determine growth areas for each level of mastery. What may be the cause? Create an instuctional plan.				
1.0-1.5 - Data Point 1	1.0-1.5 - Data Point 2	1.0-1.5 - Data Point 3	1.0-1.5 - Data Point 4	1.0-1.5 - Data Point 5
Growth Areas	Growth Areas	Growth Areas	Growth Areas	Growth Areas
INstructional plan	Instructional plan	Instructional Plan	Instructional Plan	Instructional Plan
2.0-2.5 - Data Point 1	2.0-2.5 - Data Point 2	2.0-2.5 - Data Point 3	2.0-2.5 - Data Point 4	2.0-2.5 - Data Point 5
Growth Areas	Growth Areas	Growth Areas	Growth Areas	Growth Areas
Instructional plan	Instructional plan	Instructional Plan	Instructional Plan	Instructional Plan
3.0-3.5 - Data Point 1	3.0-3.5 - Data Point 2	3.0-3.5 - Data Point 3	3.0-3.5 - Data Point 4	3.0-3.5 - Data Point 5
Growth Areas	Growth Areas	Growth Areas	Growth Areas	Growth Areas
Instructional plan	Instructional plan	Instructional Plan	Instructional Plan	Instructional Plan
4.0 - Data Point 1	4.0 - Data Point 2	4.0 - Data Point 3	4.0 - Data Point 4	4.0 - Data Point 5
Growth Areas	Growth Areas	Growth Areas	Growth Areas	Growth Areas
Instructional plan	Instructional plan	Instructional Plan	Instructional Plan	Instructional Plan

4. Based on your data and the plan you created above, what are we commiting to as a team, and what do each of us commit to individually?	
Team Commitments (What will we do to ensure our plan is implemented?)	Individual Commitments (Round Robin Discussion - what will I do to ensure that the plan is implemented?)

TARGET:								
Key		1	1.5	2	2.5	3	3.5	4
Teacher A								Teacher B
Student								Student

Teacher A								Teacher B						
4					#DIV/0!	#DIV/0!	#DIV/0!	4	#DIV/0!	#DIV/0!	#DIV/0!	#DIV/0!	#DIV/0!	#DIV/0!
3.5	#DIV/0!	#DIV/0!	#DIV/0!	#DIV/0!	#DIV/0!	#DIV/0!		3.5	#DIV/0!	#DIV/0!	#DIV/0!	#DIV/0!	#DIV/0!	#DIV/0!
3	#DIV/0!	#DIV/0!	#DIV/0!	#DIV/0!	#DIV/0!	#DIV/0!		3	#DIV/0!	#DIV/0!	#DIV/0!	#DIV/0!	#DIV/0!	#DIV/0!
2.5	#DIV/0!	#DIV/0!	#DIV/0!	#DIV/0!	#DIV/0!	#DIV/0!		2.5	#DIV/0!	#DIV/0!	#DIV/0!	#DIV/0!	#DIV/0!	#DIV/0!
2	#DIV/0!	#DIV/0!	#DIV/0!	#DIV/0!	#DIV/0!	#DIV/0!		2	#DIV/0!	#DIV/0!	#DIV/0!	#DIV/0!	#DIV/0!	#DIV/0!
1.5	#DIV/0!	#DIV/0!	#DIV/0!	#DIV/0!	#DIV/0!	#DIV/0!		1.5	#DIV/0!	#DIV/0!	#DIV/0!	#DIV/0!	#DIV/0!	#DIV/0!
1	#DIV/0!	#DIV/0!	#DIV/0!	#DIV/0!	#DIV/0!	#DIV/0!		1	#DIV/0!	#DIV/0!	#DIV/0!	#DIV/0!	#DIV/0!	#DIV/0!

Figure 2: Data conversation tool used in District 96 to show students' level of mastery. Used with permission.

HIGH IMPACT STRATEGIES

Provide a Variety of Assessments

Monitoring our students' progress is a priority, and we strive to assess our students formally and informally during each lesson. We start designing CFAs with the end goal in mind, then create assessment opportunities throughout the unit. This design ensures that we have a thorough understanding of what each student knows and is able to do as well as the areas in which students can benefit from additional support. Each assessment yields diagnostic data that gives us critical information about how the student is progressing in their learning of the content and language targets and how to move forward to ensure successful academic and linguistic growth. On the following page are the types of assessments we use in the classroom, along with their purposes and reflections on what they mean for our personal and pedagogical practice.

Think of SWIRL to Create Opportunities for Assessment Across Content Areas

When we first started creating opportunities for assessment, we felt like we were assessing everything! The truth is, we were. Whether it was an observation, a formative assessment, or a benchmark assessment, we were always learning about students through their work, interactions, and behaviors. The more we knew about the students, the more meaningful the lessons

became. Realistically, the students don't know they are being assessed most of the time. The majority of the planned assessments are informal check-ins with all or some of the students. To get the most out of an assessment, we plan for instruction making sure that the students are SWIRLing—speaking, writing, interacting, reading, and listening—during each lesson. When these instructional components are in place, you will have multiple opportunities for data collection. We know that we need data from across all content areas and settings, and this data needs to be collected frequently so we can better shift instruction in real-time. We have found our Literacy Unit Planning Tool (Figure 3, p. 83) helpful to do this effectively. It can be used daily, weekly, or as a unit planning tool. In this example, the tool is used to help brainstorm the targets, skills, strategies, scaffolds, activities, and assessments in one subject area for a full unit.

Use Backward Planning for the Unit to Ensure Both Language and Content Are Being Assessed and Analyzed

Inspired by the four critical questions of a PLC (DuFour et al., 2010) and the work of Grant Wiggins and Jay McTighe (2012) in Understanding by Design, we backward plan instruction to have a clear understanding of the unit goals. We found that if we strictly follow the teacher's manual and plan day by day, we rarely see the big picture. Lessons may be somewhat unsystematic or disjointed, and so inevitably, they might seem disconnected to students as well. On the other hand, when we look

TYPE OF ASSESSMENT	PURPOSE	PERSONAL REFLECTIONS
Observing Students	To describe students' participation in the learning process (knowledge, skills, language practice, interaction with other students)	-Is great for collecting listening and speaking data -Is very informal so kids don't feel pressure to perform -Can be with the whole class or just a few kids
Conferring With Students	To identify students' current knowledge of the content, possible misconceptions, and emerging language practice	-Helps you learn a lot about how students think -Builds your relationship with the students -Enables you to give language supports as needed -Helps build the capacity of the teacher when a coach models how to confer with students or engages in co-conferring with students
Entrance Slips	To gain insights into students' prior knowledge and background experience as well as their unique ways of expressing their ideas	-Are great for splitting the group based on current knowledge **before** a lesson starts -Can add variety by pairing students with the same ability or different abilities on the current skill -Can inform an in-the-moment decision about whether you need to build background knowledge before teaching
Exit Slips	To identify students' current knowledge of the content, possible misconceptions, and emerging language practice after instruction has ended	-Are a great way to see if students understood the lesson -Provide data to plan for small-group intervention -Provide data to differentiate for the next time you teach that target or skill
Common Formative Assessments	To assess a group of students with the same tools so that teachers can identify patterns of content learning and language use	-Ensure *all* students are held to the same expectations -Can be teacher-created to be more meaningful to your needs -Enable amazing conversations about student trends — *don't skip that part!*
Benchmark Assessments (Can Be Summative)	To identify students' understanding of skills and language after significant instruction — this *may* guide future instruction	-Are useful before a unit starts to see what the students will be assessed on -Are great as a reflection tool for students and teachers

at the unit lessons prior to teaching, we not only understand the larger goals of the unit but also get a sense of how the lessons connect and how we can make these connections as we teach. When backward planning, we ask ourselves these questions:

- What do the students need to know and be able to do academically and linguistically? What are the goals of the unit?

- How will we know if they are success-ful? What assessments will show us that the students are successful?

- What will we do if students are not successful yet? How will we intervene?

- What will we do if students have already learned the material after the first round of instruction? How will we extend the learning?

We answer these questions before planning a unit and examine them again when planning for each lesson. (See Planning Template Tool on p. 85)

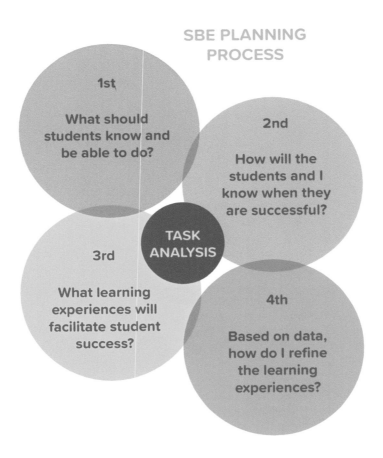

SBE PLANNING PROCESS

1st
What should students know and be able to do?

2nd
How will the students and I know when they are successful?

TASK ANALYSIS

3rd
What learning experiences will facilitate student success?

4th
Based on data, how do I refine the learning experiences?

> If a student transferred from one school to another, all of the same expectations were in place.

● ● ●

SUCCESS STORIES

Jackie shares a story about how she led the district-wide, fifth-grade team in collaboratively scoring a writing assessment. Notice how much time the team spent making sure all teachers were familiar with the rubric and consistent with their grading.

Throughout our district, assessing student work across grade-level teams is a priority. Teachers analyze a variety of student work and determine what an expected response should look like, not only at their own school but district-wide. At the end of the last trimester, all of the fifth-grade teachers in the district came together to collaboratively score a writing assessment, and I facilitated the meeting. The first part of the agenda was to review the district-created rubric to ensure we all knew the expectations for scoring at mastery, developing, and extending levels. We all had a chance to ask questions or clarify what something meant on the rubric. After everyone had a common understanding of the expectations, we looked at one student's paper and

individually graded it. When there were discrepancies about the score the student should receive on a given target, the team discussed how and why they scored the student the way they did. All teachers got to voice their opinions and give the reasons they'd graded in a certain way. We discussed the different perspectives and came to a consensus.

As we examined each item, we referred to the rubric to guarantee we were being objective. This ensured that all students would be held to the same expectations, and we were not lowering our expectations for some. Once we had collaboratively scored one paper, we moved on to another and continued until we all confidently understood what a mastery paper should include for each target. Teachers left with both a better understanding of their students' work and future instructional ideas based on our collaborative conversations. The amazing part of this whole process was that all students in the district were being assessed in the same manner. If a student transferred from one school to another, all of the same expectations were in place. The district-wide teacher collaboration took subjective grading out of the picture. Students were scored only on the work they produced.

Jackie recounts how she and one of her co-teachers explored new ways to assess students informally to gather more data that would help them maximize their instructional time. Notice how Jackie and her co-teacher move through the planning template while thinking of the lesson structure. The data collected was authentic, and the students didn't realize they were being assessed.

During one of our co-planning meetings, my co-teacher and I started talking about how we wanted more diagnostic data to help us support students at a high level. We already had a lot of formal assessments that our district provided for us, and now we were looking for informal ways to collect data from authentic student work. We started by listing all of the ways we could think of to assess our students, with the hopes of getting to know them better academically and linguistically. Our list was *long*! Some of the ideas included:

- making observations with a premade checklist,
- using FlipGrid or Seesaw,
- writing on their desks,
- listening to conversations,
- writing letters to people in the class or building,
- making presentations,
- asking student leaders to help lead lessons, and
- assigning exit and entrance slips using Pear Deck, etc.

We knew we had a plethora of options to choose from, so we selected a few to start with to focus our attention. We chose to observe students using a premade checklist, to have students use FlipGrid to respond to questions, and to listen to conversations. All of these options would give us assessment data on academic and language growth in listening, speaking, reading, and writing.

With these activities in mind, my co-teacher and I sat down to look at an upcoming lesson. The goal of the lesson was to describe a character and tell how that character's actions contributed to a sequence of events. We decided we wanted the students to speak their answers aloud, so we chose to use FlipGrid as the informal assessment activity for the students. Since we also wanted the students to answer in complete sentences, we made sure to include in the directions a previously taught strategy for answering in complete sentences called Turn the Question Around (TTQA). We anticipated some students would need a little support, so we also had sentence starters for those who wanted or needed them. We also wanted to remind the students of the anchor chart of character traits we made on the wall in our classroom. We knew the students were successful if they could answer the questions correctly in a complete sentence. Now that we had talked through the whole lesson, we were ready to teach.

After the students came into class, we told them they would do a FlipGrid based on the reading for the day. They had to record themselves answering the questions and respond to two other people's grids. They loved listening to others and adding silly faces to their pictures when they were finished responding. Before they had to speak into FlipGrid, students were given time to plan their responses on paper. While the students were planning or recording, my co-teacher and I walked around and noticed who needed support. We answered quick questions for some, and for others who were really struggling, we pulled a small group and did the activity together.

After the lesson, we planned a time to meet and listen to the FlipGrids together. We had our grade books open while we listened, and we logged the grades right then. We also noted who was in our small groups that needed extra support. Those students would come to an intervention group to practice the target again until they were comfortable on their own. Other students who didn't answer the question correctly or didn't use a complete sentence would also join a small group for intervention. We immediately had the data we needed to intervene, both now and for the next time this target cycled back. We could even differentiate the subsequent lesson based on these answers.

Below is how we completed the lesson plan template for this lesson. Based on this experience, we are considering adding a final column to capture our collaborative analysis of student work.

DATE:				
Target: *What do we want students to know and be able to do?*	**Skills:** *What modality will the students be working in? (SWIRL)*	**Strategies:** *What method will help students learn the desired target?*	**Scaffolds:** *What supports are needed for students in order to enhance learning and aid in the mastery of tasks?*	**Activities:** *How will the students practice the skill?*
Describe a character and tell how their actions contribute to the sequence of events	Speaking: Describing a character verbally in a complete sentence	Turn the Question Around'	Sentence starters, word bank of character traits on an anchor chart	Record a video on the app FlipGrid
Assessments: *How will you know if the students are successful with the target or activity?* If they can answer both parts of the question in complete sentences				

Main Topic-68 Ways

Please answer the question below and provide details from the text to support your answer.

Your Name *

Short answer text

:::

What is the Main Topic of pages 18-19? Give at least 1 detail from the text to support your answer.

Long answer text

Stephanie shares how she and one of her co-teachers used entrance slips to determine baseline data to differentiate instruction for students and exit slips to see how the students grew after a lesson.

In a fifth-grade classroom, my co-teacher and I were planning for our whole group instruction and determined that our focus needed to be on the skill of identifying a theme. As we were looking at our most recent data, we determined there were three different groups of students. The first group had shown us three or more data points indicating that they were mastering this skill, the second group showed three or more data points indicating that they had not, and the third group's data points were inconsistent. We decided that, for this lesson, we would split the class based on entrance slip results. We then identified who would be working with my co-teacher to extend the target (the students already mastering), who would be working with me to learn a new strategy to identify the theme (the students consistently not showing mastery), and who we needed to be sure to check in with and place according

to their entrance slip responses (the students with inconsistent previous data).

After collecting the completed entrance slips, the two of us came together, quickly went through our data, and finalized the two groups. By the end of the lesson, the students in my co-teacher's group partnered up with the students in my group and supported them in using the new strategy I had taught, as well as giving insight into what was working best for them. That evening for homework, we gave the students an exit slip to identify the theme of a story. When my co-teacher and I met to co-assess the exit slips, we were pleased to see that seven out of the ten students who were once not showing mastery were now successfully mastering the target of identifying the theme. We also determined that overall, seven out of the eight Culturally and Linguistically Diverse (CLD) students in the class were now mastering. The one student who wasn't currently mastering had still shown growth and had moved from not mastering the skill to developing it instead.

●●● CONCLUSION

Assessments truly are the core of instruction. Continually collecting data, collaborating with team members around the data trends, and planning instruction based on the needs of the students will help students achieve at high levels. Monitoring student progress allows the teacher to fully understand students' needs and plan for differentiated instruction. The three essential strategies for designing quality assessments are 1) using a variety of assessments, 2) using SWIRL as multiple opportunities for assessment of student learning, and 3) utilizing backward planning. When these high impact strategies are embedded into the assessment cycle, teachers will have a clear understanding of their students' current knowledge and possible misconceptions. This data collection allows teachers to instruct in a way that enables students to achieve their maximum potential.

PLANNING TEMPLATE TOOL

LITERACY UNIT PLANNING TOOL					
Target(s): What do we want students to know and be able to do?	**Skills:** What modality will the students be working in? (SWIRL)	**Strategies:** What method will help students learn the desired target?	**Scaffolds:** What supports are needed for students in order to enhance learning and aid in the mastery of tasks?	**Activities:** How will the students practice the skill?	**Assessment:** How will you know if the students are successful with the target or activity?

Figure 3: Incomplete planning tool used for one content area unit

TARGET: What do we want students to know and be able to do?			
Skills: What modality will the students be working in? (SWIRL)	**Strategies:** What method will help students learn the desired target?	**Scaffolds:** What supports are needed for students in order to enhance learning and aid in the mastery of tasks?	**Activities:** How will the students practice the skill?
Assessment: How will we know if students are successful?			

Figure 4: Incomplete planning tool used for one target

TARGET: What do we want students to know and be able to do? Lit 1 (T1, T2, T3): Quote accurately from a text when explaining what the text says explicitly and when drawing inferences from the text.

Skills: What modality will the students be working in? (SWIRL)	**Strategies:** What method will help students learn the desired target?	**Scaffolds:** What supports are needed for students in order to enhance learning and aid in the mastery of tasks?	**Activities:** How will the students practice the skill?
1. Navigate fifth-grade level text 2. Analyze a prompt or question 3. Identify what the text says explicitly and paraphrase the information 4. Make inferences 5. Pull relevant quotes (extends: strongest key details) 6. Know how to format quote(s) from the text appropriately 7. Support the chosen quote(s) with a response that shows understanding of why the details are chosen	• Apply "Important vs. Interesting" to fiction text • 4 step process for paraphrasing • Readers Explain Their Thinking • Text Clue/ Background Knowledge Addition	• Sentence frames • Prove it with text evidence anchor chart • RACE to support students in structuring their response R= Restate the question A = Answer the question C = Cite text evidence E = Explain what it means • Formatting quotes	• Detective activity • Fan-N-Pick (Kagan, 2009) Role 1: Fan Role 2: Pick & Read Role 3: Answer question with a quotation Role 4: Explain why Role 3 chose that quote by saying, "That quote supports the question by____" (or can disagree and explain why another quote is stronger)

Assessment: How will you know if the students are successful with the target or activity?

*__Speaking/Interacting:__ Answering in complete sentences, agreeing or disagreeing with their partner in complete sentences using "because"

*__Writing:__ Quoting the text accurately, using the RACE strategy to answer the question in a paragraph

*__Reading:__ After reading the text, the student can answer comprehension questions

*__Listening/Interacting:__ After listening to their partner, they can agree or disagree with their answer

Figure 5: Sample completed planning tool used for one specific target.

WEEK OF:						
	Target(s): What do we want students to know and be able to do?	**Skills:** What modality will the students be working in? (SWIRL)	**Strategies:** What method will help students learn the desired target?	**Scaffolds:** What supports are needed for students in order to enhance learning and aid in the mastery of tasks?	**Activities:** How will the students practice the skill?	**Assessment:** How will you know if the students are successful with the target or activity?
Literacy						
Math						
Science						
Social Studies						

Figure 6: Incomplete planning tool used for multiple subjects
Created by Stephanie Just in collaboration with Kildeer 96 teachers. Used with permission.

References and Further Resources

DuFour, R., DuFour, R., Eaker, R., & Many, T. (2010). *Learning by doing: A handbook for professional learning communities at work*. Solution Tree.

Kagan, S., & Kagan, M. (2009). *Cooperative learning.* Kagan Publishing

McTighe, J., & Wiggins, G. P. (2012). Understanding by design framework [White Paper]. ASCD. https://www.ascd.org/ASCD/pdf/siteASCD/publications/UbD_WhitePaper0312.pdf

Cultivating
Collaboration
WITH MULTIPLE TEAMS

Katie Toppel

Durham Elementary School is a public, Title I school in the Tigard-Tualatin School District in Oregon. There are approximately 550 students, and 24 different languages are spoken among its students and their families. Approximately 200 of those students attend kindergarten and first grade, and nearly 25 percent of kindergarteners and 20 percent of first graders are identified as English learners (ELs). I am one of two English language development specialists in the building, and I collaborate and co-teach with eight classroom teachers across kindergarten and first grade.

Ideally, if content and grade-level teams spend more time at the beginning of the year engaging in long-term planning, they will not need to spend as much time working to prepare for collaboration meetings throughout the school year.

SETTING THE STAGE

For the past several years, K-1 grade-level teachers and I have been incorporating teacher collaboration and co-teaching to better align content and language instruction. We shifted to this model to serve English learners and provide language support in the context of what students are already learning as opposed to removing them from classrooms for isolated language development lessons. We strongly feel that our youngest ELs benefit more from staying in their general education classrooms to receive integrated language instruction rather than leaving their learning communities to receive language instruction in a separate setting. We have grown in our confidence that all of our students, English learners and those who are not, benefit from explicit language instruction tied to literacy, content learning, and writing. In our current system, we have one part-time English language teacher supporting four kindergarten classes and four first-grade classes. Our school was one of a few within the district to pioneer co-teaching within a predominantly pullout system, but collaboration and co-teaching are now being embraced and expanded on a broader level. Our school district, under new Title III leadership, is working to establish systematized expectations and practices so that more English learners can benefit from the convergence of content and language instruction as well as the positive impacts of teacher collaboration.

From the outset, we have intentionally created a thread through literacy content, oracy practice, and writing so that students speak, write, interact, read, and listen (SWIRL) in every lesson. Technology is also selectively and intentionally utilized as a tool to support practice in the four language domains. We structure lessons using the gradual release of responsibility model (Fisher & Frey, 2013)—focused instruction, guided practice, collaborative learning, and independent learning—so that lessons are frontloaded with explicit language instruction, which leads to shared language practice and ends with independent writing. Language content is supported with visuals, including photos, clip art, and slide decks, to provide comprehensible input (Echevarría, Vogt, & Short, 2017).

We practice the target language in a whole group setting with teacher modeling, and then students practice it in alternating turns or conversations with their partners. We incorporate a lot of songs, chants, and repetition so students have many opportunities to practice the target language, with teacher-led support, with classmates, and then independently with visual support/reminders. Partner talk is structured using the QSSSA (question, stem, signal, share, assess) strategy (Seidlitz & Perryman, 2021) to ensure that all students are accountable to respond while providing think time before they have to engage with peers. We also use equity sticks—which have the names of individual students written on them—to randomly select a few students or partners to demonstrate target language for the rest of the class as a way to

	Lesson	Phonics	Word(s)	Theme	Literacy	Writing	Science/Health/	Social Studies	Looking Ahead
Sept 3-6	Kinder Connect Meetings								
Sept 9-13	1	m s a t c		Rhymes	Start Alphabet Bootcamp (teach daily letter sound for 26 days), Alphafriends chant			Classroom Routines	
Sept 16-20	2	p j n f b		Rhymes				Classroom Routines	
Sept 23-27	Unit 1 1	l g r d h	I	Families				Classroom Routines Jog-a-thon	
Sept 30-Oct. 4	2	o x e k v	like	School				Assessments	
Oct 7-10 (4) F Inservice	3	u l z y	the	Pet					
Oct 14-18	4	m	and	Jobs	Explicitly teach "letter of week" jobs so students will be independent for later seat work. **Start sounding out CVC words.**		magnets		
Oct 21-24 (4) F Training		q w	*by*		finish Alphabet Bootcamp		pumpkins		
Oct 28-Nov 1	5	s, -ing	*so*	Helping			slugs and snails / stone soup & bread	**Halloween on Wednesday**	
Nov 4-7 (4) F Work Day	Unit 2 6	a	see	Senses	start CVC whole word rdg.	I like apples. The best is applesauce/apple cider/apple pie/apple slices.	apples, applesauce	Veterans/Patriotic Activities	
Nov 12-15 (4) M holiday	7	t	we	Sounds & Languages	lined dictation paper (CVC, sight word sent.)	I like toys. The best is ____. It is	tall towers (marshmallows and toothpicks)		
Nov 18-22		th	*that*					Thanksgiving Activities	Send Home Gingerbread house letter
Thanksgiving Week									
Dec 2-6	8	c	a, *on*	Move		I like cookies. The best is ____. It is	candy canes/ choc chip cookies		

Figure 1: Curriculum map detailing content topics and themes, weekly letters and sight words, and special events shared by a kindergarten team

informally assess. When students move into independent writing, they can use the visual supports from the lesson to scaffold their writing process. They also have visual and linguistic scaffolds built into their Seesaw activities, which they access on their iPads.

Because we advocated to implement the collaboration and co-teaching model before it was truly a district initiative, and without formal training, we have had to figure out how to make it work. Over time, we have come to appreciate certain practices and tools as being instrumental to our success. One of those tools, which both the kindergarten and first-grade teams created, is a year-long curriculum guide. The documents my teams developed include week-by-week information about content topics and literacy themes, noting which lessons will be addressed from the prescribed reading curricula. Figure 1 shows an example of a curriculum map detailing content topics and themes, weekly letters and sight words, and special events shared by a kindergarten team. Before we collaborate, I am able to preview the curriculum guide and the digital reading curriculum to anticipate what content will be undertaken in the subsequent week(s). Knowing the areas of content focus and standards in advance allows me to consider what language forms, functions, targets, or objectives align with the content. For the most part, because teams have provided me with detailed documents that outline the scope and sequence for content delivery and access to digital teacher manuals, I do not need to consult with grade-level teachers for any of my personal preplanning. I can come to meetings with a good foundational understanding of what grade-level teams will be working on, prepared to share ideas for incorporating language instruction. Over time, we have learned that it's helpful to agree on the lessons' content and language objectives to streamline the co-planning process and maximize the use of our co-planning time.

Because I know the lesson focus in advance, I can prepare for co-planning meetings by drafting visuals and gathering supplementary materials. Even if I am not entirely sure classroom teachers will want to move forward with my suggested ideas, I still take the time to prepare visuals—or at least sketch them out—so my co-teachers can get a clear picture of what I have in mind. I lay out materials in pocket charts, hanging charts and posters, and make copies of documents so classroom teachers can see what lesson materials look like and better visualize how language instruction will play out. This also maximizes the amount of work we can accomplish because seeing the materials prevents the need for extended explanation.

When we first began our journey into collaboration and co-teaching, most of our lessons were the same across different classrooms. Now, however, I customize many elements of the lessons, including lesson delivery and the co-teaching models used to deliver instruction for individual teachers and their students. Across classrooms, teachers differ in their preferred graphic organizers, classroom management techniques, methods for grouping students, and ways of emphasizing writing versus speaking when retelling, as well as their readiness for technology integration. Teachers also have different comfort levels with the various co-teaching models and even with co-teaching itself. I am extra conscious of ensuring the changes I make reflect the environment I am in. At times

it can be challenging to keep track of the distinct ways teachers and classrooms operate. Yet I recognize that, as a specialist entering into many different classrooms that have established rules, procedures, and communities, I need to be flexible. Technology is a particular area in which integration across classrooms is unique. One great benefit of co-teaching is that I can observe how one co-teacher utilizes technology, then take what I have learned and support another teacher in integrating that same technology. We are continuously sharing best practices across classrooms because collaboration allows us to learn from one another.

When we first started co-teaching, all of our planning was done remotely using a combination of email and Google Docs. However, face-to-face collaboration has made a huge difference in our ability to work together collectively and contribute equitably. During a typical co-planning session, we follow an agenda to make sure we cover all the things we need to discuss in our limited time together. We take a look at the weekly schedule to see what school events (holidays, field trips, fire drills, assemblies, etc.) may interfere with our regular co-teaching schedule, and if needed, we adjust our schedule to reflect the time we will have in that particular week. We address each content area we'll cover together, and I present ideas for incorporating language. This is when I ask for feedback from the content teachers, and they can ask questions and gain clarity on language integration. I take notes on their ideas and suggestions for the language objectives and then we discuss lesson ideas.

As we are talking, I make a list of action items that I need to complete prior to our lessons and the action items classroom teachers need to accomplish in their post-planning. I have a hard time remembering information that is not written down, and I always strive to be organized and efficient when working with my co-teachers. Therefore, I try to leave meetings with a clear list of what I need to achieve during my individual post-planning so I will be prepared for lessons the following week and be able to get materials to teachers before the lessons they will teach on their own. I want to ensure that, if I have agreed to create something or do something, I am true to my word and follow through. Establishing and building trust is very important for collaborative partnerships, so I always want to make sure I am reliable and honor our agreements.

Once I have reflected independently, I email my teams, detailing what we decided on and what action items need to be completed in order to prepare for our lessons. I find it helpful to restate or summarize what we talked about, which is also helpful for any team members who were unable to attend the meeting due to IEP meetings or absences. I try to complete lesson plans within two days of our co-planning session and send them to teams along with any clarifying questions that have surfaced so that classroom teachers have their plans in advance.

BLUEPRINT

Co-planning with teams requires preparation, organization, and clear communication. Having systems to support these elements is essential for making sure collaborative planning operates smoothly. The following blueprint outlines ideas for supporting successful collaboration with multiple teams.

Utilize Long-Term Planning to Organize Content Themes, Topics, and Lessons

Curriculum guides or unit maps are valuable tools for organizing the instructional scope and sequence of lessons in order to have a clear plan for teaching. These tools provide language teachers with an outline of upcoming content and can include content standards, topics, themes, vocabulary, and information about assignments. Language teachers can preview the information, organize their ideas around what language forms and functions align with the upcoming instruction, and prepare suggestions to share during team collaboration. If teachers/schools use a prescribed or packaged curriculum, there may be less of a need to create a curriculum map, because the scope and sequence is already established within the curriculum itself. However, providing the language specialist with access to the teachers' manuals or digital curriculum will also ensure that they have sufficient knowledge of upcoming content to plan for language and literacy instruction.

Set a Regular Time to Co-plan as a Group

Regular collaboration meetings are essential for successful teaching partnerships. As such, scheduling a consistent time to come together as a team is imperative. Weekly meetings work well; however, some teams prefer to tackle planning for larger instructional chunks with monthly or unit planning. Regardless of the frequency, the length of collaborative work sessions should be sufficient for the amount of instructional content or number of lessons being covered.

Maximize Preparation and Organization

Preplanning, or preparing to collaborate, can take place independently (Dove & Honigsfeld, 2018). Therefore, it is helpful for content teachers to frontload the sharing of unit/curriculum guides, curriculum materials, or expectations for accessing materials as needed so that language teachers can conduct their preplanning responsibilities independently. Preparation prior to collaboration and co-planning is a helpful step to ensure that teams can focus on a manageable number of actionable items when they come together rather than starting entirely from square one. Co-planning meetings may be the only shared time co-teachers have to collaborate with one another, meaning content teachers may not be able to use additional time outside of the meetings to provide language specialists the necessary information about upcoming instruction. The more information language specialists have upfront, the more self-sufficient they can be in preparing to collaborate with colleagues and maximizing productivity during those meetings.

Establish Content Alignment without Mandating Instructional Delivery

When language specialists collaborate and/or co-teach with a large number of content and classroom teachers, it's challenging to balance the individuality of partnerships and uniqueness of student groups with the scheduling requirements for co-planning lessons with so many different teachers. It is helpful when grade-level teams or those that teach the same content area align their instructional topics, themes, or units in order to streamline the co-planning process and maximize time. This does not mean that all co-teaching teams or teachers carry out the exact same lessons; rather, there should be agreement on what will be taught but not necessarily *how* it will be taught. Making co-planned and co-taught lessons cookie-cutter across all classrooms simply for convenience is never a good idea. There is no one-size-fits-all approach for collaboration and co-teaching.

Use a Meeting Agenda to Create Clarity around Action Items

In order to stay organized and use the time allotted for collaboration meetings efficiently, teams can devise an agenda. Following an agenda helps ensure that teams can address everything they need to within the designated meeting time. Teachers are busy, and time is a most precious commodity, so sticking to a plan helps everyone feel their time is valued and used well. An agenda also helps prevent teams from running out of time and leaving the meeting with a lot of loose ends or without a sense of closure. Teams should designate a notetaker during meetings to document what was discussed and what decisions were made, particularly if any team members could not attend due to absences, professional development, or other obligations, such as IEP meetings. The notetaker can send a meeting recap to all team members, including agreed-upon action items so each person knows their post-planning responsibilities.

Utilize Digital Tools to Share, Collaborate on Lesson Plans, and Communicate

If all of the details are not settled in the co-planning session, co-teaching pairs can utilize other ways to connect that don't necessarily require additional meeting time. Emails, texts, and Google Docs are convenient ways to pose and answer questions, confer, and make decisions that provide both partners flexibility in terms of when and from where they respond. It's ideal to establish both expectations and boundaries around communication with co-teachers to ensure all parties are on the same page. For some teachers, receiving a text after school hours requesting clarification about a lesson would not be a problem. For others, it might seem like an invasion of personal or family time. Co-teaching agreements are a great tool to create jointly in order to better understand partners and communicate effectively.

HIGH IMPACT STRATEGIES

Of all the ideas presented in the blueprint for success, a few stand out as being the most critical for fostering organization, efficiency, and communication. These high impact strategies also represent a great place for teachers to start if they are new to collaborating with multiple teams.

Maximize Preparation before Collaboration

If both content teachers and language teachers engage in preplanning (i.e., preparation in advance of the co-planning meeting), the team will be better prepared to make the most of collaboration time. Engaging in collaborative partnerships does require classroom and content teachers to be a step ahead in planning and organization, which may seem challenging or daunting. However, these efforts will be hugely beneficial to all team members when they work together to plan for instruction with both a language and content lens. Ideally, if content and grade-level teams spend more time at the beginning of the year engaging in long-term planning, they will not need to spend as much time working to prepare for collaboration meetings throughout the school year.

ACTION ITEMS FOR PREPLANNING

Grade-Level/ Content Teacher Teams

- Align scope and sequence for the content area(s)
- Create curriculum maps for months, units, or the year
- Share curriculum map(s) with the EL specialist

Language Teacher

- Draft language objectives
- Plan for differentiation across language levels
- Draft visuals, collect supplementary materials in advance
- Consider the best co-teaching models for upcoming lessons
- Consider how to support students in building background
- Think about how to incorporate all four language domains in lessons

Content teachers may prefer to navigate the year by planning one unit at a time, which requires anticipating and planning one unit while teaching another. In this case, it is imperative to give the language specialists enough headway for sufficient preplanning time prior to co-planning meetings. All team members will be able to contribute ideas during the co-planning sessions; however, it is beneficial for content teachers when language specialists anticipate what can be done to support ELs and come prepared to share those ideas and strategies. In some circumstances, the language specialist will be co-delivering the instruction with content teachers. In others, teachers may be collaborating only to plan, and the content teachers will deliver both content and language instruction based on the ideas and plans generated during team collaboration.

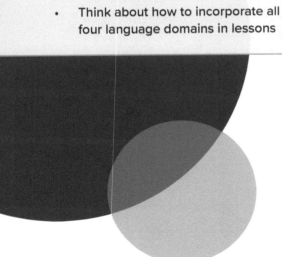

As part of the preplanning process, the team can outline or draft many parts of the lesson plan. The elements in Figure 2 highlighted in orange represent information that should be included in a curriculum guide. The elements highlighted in purple are ones that the language teacher can think about and draft prior to the co-planning meeting.

Create Common Lesson Objectives with Modifications for Each Classroom

When content teams or grade-level teams agree on a scope and sequence, language specialists can collaborate with teams rather than individuals. This reduces the difficulty in planning around language specialists' schedules. During the co-planning meeting, teams can work through and discuss the alignment of content and language as well as how to differentiate for students at different levels of proficiency in English. Content teachers and language specialists can dialogue around which co-teaching models will be used (if applicable), how students will be grouped, and what activities will be used to incorporate all four of the language domains. Sometimes, lessons might look pretty similar across different classrooms, meaning there is general consensus among team members about lesson features.

GRADE/LESSON FOCUS		
Content Standards: ELP Standards:	Content Objective: Language Objective: Language Form: Language Function:	Sentence Frames: Key Vocabulary: Adaptation of Content: Emerging: Progressing:

Co-Teaching Model:
Supplementary Materials/Visuals:
Building Background:
   Connection to Prior Learning:
   Connection to Students' Experiences:
Lesson Sequence:
Practice & Application:
Grouping Configuration:
Review/Assessment:		

Figure 2: Adapted from Echevarría, J., Vogt, M. E., & Short, D. (2017). *Making content comprehensible for English learners: The SIOP® model* (5th ed.). Pearson.

During co-planning, teachers come to a consensus around key lesson elements, yet many other components remain flexible and depend on the needs of particular teachers and their students. The elements in Figure 3 highlighted in purple represent parts of the lesson that educators should discuss when collaborating.

Alignment of content and language objectives provides instructional consistency across classrooms; yet many elements of the lessons—including lesson delivery and the types of activities used for interaction, practice, and application—can differ from classroom to classroom. Across classrooms, teachers have unique instructional and management styles, different procedures and routines, and varied structures and expectations for grouping, as well as individual readiness for technology integration. Teachers also have disparate comfort levels with the various co-teaching models and co-teaching itself. For all of these reasons, despite common content and language objectives, lessons can look different across multiple classrooms. If preferences for grouping, activities, and co-teaching models differ greatly among teachers, individual instructors may need to spend additional time corresponding with the language specialist about the particular details of lessons that will take place in

GRADE/LESSON FOCUS		
Content Standards: **ELP Standards:**	Content Objective: Language Objective: Language Form: Language Function:	Sentence Frames: Key Vocabulary: **Adaptation of Content:** Emerging: Progressing:

Co-Teaching Model:
Supplementary Materials/Visuals:
Building Background:
   Connection to Prior Learning:
   Connection to Students' Experiences:
Lesson Sequence:
Practice & Application:
Grouping Configuration:
Review/Assessment:		

Figure 3: Adapted from Echevarría, J., Vogt, M. E., & Short, D. (2017). *Making content comprehensible for English learners: The SIOP® model* (5th ed.). Pearson.

their classrooms. Team co-planning time may or may not include sufficient time to discuss and make decisions about the lesson details for each individual classroom. Admittedly, if there is a great deal of variation across classrooms, the language specialist may require more time and preparation. If this is a source of struggle or stress, co-teaching teams can work to guarantee that post-planning responsibilities are divided equitably within their partnerships.

Co-teaching agreements are a great way to establish shared expectations for working together. Identifying preferences for communication, roles and responsibilities, and boundaries can help teachers better understand how to maintain positive collaborative relationships with one another. The language specialist can take the lead in initiating conversations with each co-teaching partner around what each teacher wants and needs from the partnership. Drafting a written document is helpful to keep a record of the established agreements and intentions for future reference. Such agreements can support language teachers, in particular when they're navigating partnerships with multiple teachers or teams. They can keep track of individual teachers' preferences and adapt interactions and lessons accordingly. When a co-teaching relationship begins, teachers can also get to know one another by sharing their teaching styles, areas of strength, areas where they might seek support from each other, favorite instructional tools, or anything else that feels relevant to navigating a successful relationship.

Stay engaged and on task.

Respect Time—start on time, come prepared and end on time.

Be mindful of others when speaking your truth.

Set agenda ahead of time and stick to the agenda.

Accept consensus—validate concerns—put forth best effort to move forward.

Everyone contributes—share the air and use protocols when appropriate.

Document actions and follow up.

Organize a Meeting Agenda and Recap

Flexibility is an essential trait for co-teachers; meetings don't typically align perfectly to the agendas. However, a meeting agenda functions as a helpful structure to guide the session and keep the focus on the most essential outcomes. Consider scheduling time in the agenda to decompress or connect as friends/colleagues at the beginning of the meeting. It is also helpful to have a system for taking notes so there is a record of what was talked about and what decisions were made. One person can be in charge of taking notes for everyone, or individual teachers can take notes on their own behalf. If co-teachers have indicated different preferences for lesson delivery, it is critical for the language specialist to take good notes that organize information pertaining to particular classrooms.

Following the co-planning meeting, a designated teacher can send a recap of what was discussed and decided, particularly if any team members were unable to attend the meeting.

Action Items for Co-Planning

- Connect and build relationships among team members

- Review the weekly schedule to adjust for any holidays, field trips, fire drills, assemblies, or special events that may interfere with instruction or co-teaching

- Discuss lesson plans with attention to building background, determining lesson sequence, arranging grouping configurations, visualizing how students will interact and practice, and designing how students will be assessed

- Make team decisions about the lesson elements that will require attention during post-planning, such as necessary supplementary materials including related literature, visuals, hands-on materials, or language supports

- Review salient information and assign post-planning responsibilities for each team member

As you engage in more and more collaborative co-planning practices, you will be able to find and tweak systems to make them work for you and your colleagues. There is not a single way to co-plan correctly, but the ideas included in this chapter can surely get you going.

SUCCESS STORIES

Nasir is an English learner, born in Iraq, whose home language is Arabic. Although his parents do speak English, his dad shared that they mostly speak to the children in Arabic at home.

Nasir has an older sibling in middle school and a younger sibling in preschool. Currently in first grade, Nasir has attended school in the United States since preschool and was identified as being at level 1 proficiency in English upon entering kindergarten. Several months later, the ELPA21 language assessment also identified his language proficiency as level 1 in all four language domains. In class, Nasir smiles a lot and is eager to learn; however, at times it can be challenging to understand what he is trying to say. Among our co-teaching team, Nasir has Mrs. Parker for homeroom, Mrs. Long for reading, and myself as his English language development specialist. I collaborate with both his homeroom teacher and his reading teacher to plan lessons that foster language development. Mrs. Parker shared with me that Nasir asked her to visit his home. His younger sibling had a home visit as part of her preschool program, and he wanted to have one too. Mrs. Parker asked me if I would be interested in doing a home visit with her, and I gladly accepted.

In the short time that we visited with Nasir, his parents, and his younger sibling in their home, we learned a great deal about him that both surprised and delighted us. Nasir's dad shared with us that Nasir enjoys figuring out how things work. He will watch videos on YouTube to investigate how items can be fixed and then attempt to do so. He pulled out his parents' laptop computer and adeptly began searching for different types of video game systems to show us the one he has and the one he wants. He showed us a complicated puzzle he had put together and then asked us to play a game with him that is similar to Jenga. He strategically pulled pieces out to prevent the tower from falling and smiled from ear to ear as we each took turns. Our visit to Nasir's home was an extension of our collaborative practices, yet Mrs. Parker and I were able to process what we learned about Nasir and leverage it to plan lessons that will be meaningful for him and support his language and literacy development. We shared what we learned with Mrs. Long so that she too would have a better understanding of how to support Nasir in reading.

By no means did we have low expectations for Nasir prior to visiting his home and seeing him in his familiar environment, but now that we have accessed his personal interests and connected with his family, our overall vision for his learning has been shifted. We can find ways to engage his interest in solving puzzles and exploring by incorporating more opportunities for him to use language and literacy as it applies to higher-level thinking and challenges, and we can do so across content areas. We are eager to watch him flourish this year!

Luka is a kindergarten student who was born in Brazil and speaks Portuguese at home. He arrived in the United States a few months before he started school.

Luka is considered a newcomer because he is new to the country and, upon entering kindergarten, was evaluated at a level 1 proficiency in English. Luka started kindergarten as a silent observer, not speaking much at all but soaking in the behaviors and routines of his classroom and his peers. Luka receives co-taught language instruction alongside his peers in his regular classroom. Because we teach together, we often can more closely observe how Luka reacts to our lessons and provide one-on-one support if needed. Once, early in the school year, I tried to introduce some new words to him by having him repeat after me. Sadly, it resulted in him crying because he was not comfortable trying to say the words out loud. His classroom teacher, Mrs. Elliot, pulled him aside and used the conversation feature on Google Translate to communicate with him while I oversaw the rest of the classroom. She was able to ease his worries by telling him it was okay if he didn't understand everything while reassuring him that she and I were both there to help him. On other occasions, while Mrs. Elliot circulated among the rest of the students during partner talk time, I worked directly with Luka and his partner to support his receptive understanding with individual picture scaffolds that the rest of the students didn't need.

Over time, Luka has gained confidence and many literacy skills by learning alongside his peers. At one point, I tried to pull him out for some support, and he was resistant. Consequently, we have made an effort to keep him in the classroom because that is where he is most comfortable. Recently, he has started to use English words. He knows almost all of the letter sounds in English and reads the sight words students have learned thus far. Co-teaching provides the space to make sure we can immediately address the feelings and challenges faced by newcomers. Luka is not left to sink or swim because together as a teaching team, we can manage his needs and the needs of our other ELs and students. After six months of school, Luka demonstrated level 2 proficiency in reading, writing, and listening and level 3 proficiency in speaking on the ELPA21 summative assessment.

●●● CONCLUSION

Collaboration between a language specialist and multiple grade-level or content-area teams may seem daunting and challenging to navigate, but it doesn't have to be. Teaming becomes more manageable when systems are in place to maximize long-term content planning, assign co-planning responsibilities, and align key components of lesson preparation. When teams develop successful systems and routines, the process of collaborating can be smooth and efficient, with a sustained effort to merge content and language instruction for all students.

References and Further Resources

Cohan, A., Honigsfeld, A., & Dove, M. G. (2020). *Team up, speak up, fire up!: Educators, students, and the community working together to support English learners.* ASCD.

Davison, C. (2006). Collaboration between ESL and content teachers: How do we know when we are doing it right? *International Journal of Bilingual Education and Bilingualism, 9*(4), 454-475.

Dove, M. G., & Honigsfeld, A. (2018). *Co-teaching for English learners: A guide to collaborative planning, instruction, assessment, and reflection.* Corwin.

Echevarría, J., Vogt, M. E., & Short, D. (2017). *Making content comprehensible for English learners: The SIOP model (5th ed.).* Pearson.

Fisher, D., & Frey, N. (2013). *Better learning through structured teaching: A framework for the gradual release of responsibility.* ASCD.

Honigsfeld, A., & Dove, M. G. (2019). *Collaborating for English learners: A foundational guide for integrated practices* (2nd ed.). Corwin.

Seidlitz, J., & Perryman, B. (2021). *7 steps to a language-rich interactive classroom* (2nd ed.). Seidlitz Education.

Shin, J., Savic, V., & Machida, T. (2018). *The 6 principles for exemplary teaching of English learners: Grades K-12.* TESOL.

Zwiers, J., & Hamerla, S. R. (2017). *The K-3 guide to academic conversations: Practices, scaffolds, and activities.* Corwin.

6

Amplifying
Student &
Teacher Voice
WITH TECHNOLOGY

Michelle Gill

SNAPSHOT

I am very fortunate to support the English learners (ELs) of the Abbotsford School District.

We welcome approximately 20,000 students each year and are the eighth largest school district in British Columbia, with 30 elementary schools, seven middle schools, and seven secondary schools. Abbotsford has the third highest proportion of visible minorities among Census Metropolitan Areas in Canada. The percentage of students identified as ELs has risen in recent years, and trends suggest that this percentage will continue to increase. Supporting ELs has always been and continues to be at the forefront of the district's strategic plan. One specific goal, "Improve ethical and innovative use of technology," resonated with me in particular and would transform how I supported teachers. Providing access and an equitable playing field for all was in reach with the available technologies. The rollout of student devices across the district demonstrated its commitment to this goal.

Abbotsford School District Technology Snapshot 2017/2018		
4416 iPads	4574 PC/Laptops	4100 Chromebooks
Abbotsford School District Technology Snapshot 2020/2021		
5000 iPads	6000 PC/Laptops	4100 Chromebooks

(Chart indicates the number of devices across the Abbotsford School District.)

While the rollout of technology has increased the support for our language learners tremendously, many teachers initially didn't feel confident and weren't being intentional about the technology they were incorporating in their instruction.

SETTING THE STAGE

For years, teachers had been apprehensive about shifting to a more inclusive model of instruction where all students were supported in the same classroom. Removing some students for specialized support in another location had long been the norm. Many teachers acknowledged the benefits of a collaborative approach but were hesitant to let another professional into their classroom. They were also frustrated with the lack of dedicated co-planning time during the school day. Co-teaching and collaboration were perceived as the latest buzzwords in our district, but they lacked substance. This needed to change.

First, the district's entire curriculum and EL team engaged in some professional development: the "Art of Coaching" training (Aguilar, 2013). The goal was to have our two departments continue working in tandem to support teacher teams by creating an inclusive delivery of support. We had to model the practices we hoped our teachers would embrace. Our Director of Instruction, Perry Smith, believed

that honing our skills as coaches and strengths-based communicators would serve us well in reaching our goals. He was right. We not only learned but had the opportunity to practice a number of methods to facilitate the components of a transformational coaching conversation and develop confidence as coaches. We also brought in speakers such as Virginia Rojas, Tom Schwimmer, John Spencer, Shelley Moore, and Tan Huynh, who all acknowledged the importance of collaboration.

The belief that *all teachers were teachers of ELs* was still a shift in thinking for some of us. After advocating for structured collaboration times in schools as a way to build capacity in every teacher, the English language learner (ELL) department also dedicated weekly time at school sites to nurture effective digital practices in daily instruction.

Next, the ELL department implemented a systematic approach to support and build capacity in both our new and veteran teachers. We surveyed the EL staff using a Google Form, visited school sites, joined collaboration meetings, and talked to EL and classroom teachers one-on-one. The

Co-teaching and collaboration were perceived as the latest buzzwords in our district, but they lacked substance. This needed to change.

purpose was not to evaluate teachers but to get their feedback and learn how ELs were being integrated and supported during instructional activities. With so many effective digital platforms available to spotlight ELs' voices, we knew this was our way into the classroom. We hoped that, using technology, EL teachers would increase their students' participation in each aspect of the collaborative teaching cycle (Honigsfeld & Dove, 2010).

We examined the current co-teaching models, assessment methods, and collaborative practices at the various Abbotsford District schools. We wanted to answer several questions:

- How were teachers communicating curricular goals with their colleagues and students?

- What co-teaching models were they implementing?

- How was student progress being tracked and shared between teacher teams?

Although "innovative use of technology" and "collaboration and co-teaching" were mentioned in almost every school plan, we discovered several disappointing things:

- In a number of classrooms, collaboration and technology were not working well. A common concern was that students only had access to six shared devices in their classrooms. Teachers wanted a one-to-one model.

- During collaboration time, the bulk of the responsibility usually fell on the shoulders of one person.

- Collaboration time turned into marking, photocopying, and planning upcoming field trips.

- A large number of EL teachers felt "like a teacher's assistant rather than a teacher."

- A large number of EL teachers were implementing several high impact strategies, but they did not feel comfortable sharing them with classroom teachers.

All of this needed to change.

Guiding Keywords

The ELL department designed a three-year plan. We wanted to equip EL teachers with the skills and digital knowledge they needed to support and lead within their buildings. Four key words that would guide this change were **advocacy, equity, empowerment,** and **teamwork.** With the increasing number of diverse students entering our district, we knew teachers needed a specific skill set to address all of their "strengths and stretches." Technology would serve as the scaffolding tool that would level the playing field for all students, no matter their proficiency levels. We began conducting workshops and staff meeting presentations as soon as the school year began. Underlying the importance of advocating for the diverse needs of students, we discussed ways teachers could use technology to incorporate culturally responsive materials into their daily practices. Students needed to see themselves and their cultures reflected in classroom materials, lessons, and activities if we wanted their self-confidence and achievements to increase (Gottlieb, 2013).

The first small step was to start with books. We shared a Padlet of Diverse Books for ELs that naturally **advocate** for cultural inclusion. It allowed us to

Padlet of
Authentic Books
for ELs

demonstrate Padlet's capabilities and how it could be used in classrooms for sharing ideas, picking up resources, and increasing student collaboration. Padlet has an easy-to-use interface with intuitive features; it is essentially an online bulletin board that you can share with students or teachers by creating a link or Quick Response (QR) code. Having learned about Padlet, many teachers started to use it to structure opening activities in their classrooms. Students would use the app to respond to a question, image, or video. Since students could see their peers' ideas, it was the perfect scaffold for those who weren't quite sure what to contribute. Now they had the option to simply agree, disagree, or ask a question. This was a fantastic way to structure academic discourse. The following are additional ways teachers used Padlet in their classrooms:

- **Online Student Portfolio:** Each student had their own board, where they posted assignments, articles, and projects. Teachers commented on each one and gave meaningful feedback.

- **Vocabulary Development:** After uploading a custom background picture, teachers asked students to label the picture by posting to the wall.

- **Accessing Prior Knowledge:** Teachers posted a topic, statement, image, or video and had students comment in order to demonstrate what they knew about the topic.

- **Analyze a Quote:** Teachers presented a quote that connected to the lesson topic. Collaboratively, students discussed what they thought the quote was about.

Once the lesson and Padlet had been completed, co-teachers came together to review, assess student work, and plan their next steps.

When we talked about the term **equity**, we made it clear that it meant more than equal access to tools and resources. We wanted teachers to understand that equity meant making sure all students were exposed to high standards and had their needs met, as evidenced by outcomes and results. The building administrators with whom we worked closely already had a vision that combined student achievement and equity. We all set forth to make equitable decisions a more deliberate practice, realizing that school sites may unintentionally be exacerbating inequity by continuing practices such as placing our most at-risk students with the least experienced teachers.

A common concern we heard throughout the district was the perceived inability to support newcomers who were proficient in a language that no adult in the building spoke. We shared a free tool called Immersive Reader that had several features designed to **empower** emerging learners. Teachers were able to quickly translate content into a number of different languages. They had the option to translate the whole document or specific words. Soon, both teachers and students began using Immersive Reader to make grade-level text comprehensible. They loved browsing the dual-language picture dictionary, adjusting the rate of speech, and taking advantage of the read-aloud option. This helped nurture an inclusive classroom environment where students felt connected and like they belonged. They now had agency. This simple tool made it a bit easier to create opportunities for all students to participate and learn alongside their peers.

Another aspect we considered was how to use technology to engage the families of ELs in hopes of building community. We found that there was a sense of discomfort from both teachers and EL families. While language was the obvious roadblock, the reluctance to engage ran much deeper. Without the ability to communicate in English, and faced with trying to understand an education system that was very different from the one they had experienced, many families wondered: How could they contribute?

We turned to the free platform TalkingPoints to build a bridge to reach these families, to invite them to our **team**. It gave us the ability to connect despite the language barrier. We were able to communicate without depending on a translator or scheduling a bilingual aide to make a family phone call. At the beginning of the school year, parents were shown how to use this platform to receive auto-generated texts and audio messages in English or their native language. We gave them the opportunities to share their voices. Teachers sent photos and videos of daily classroom activities. Families were more informed and began asking more questions about school and their children's

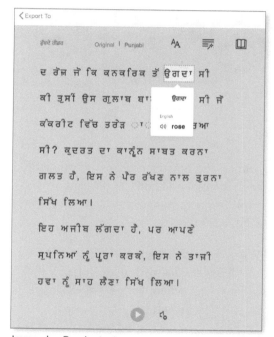

Immersive Reader text

TalkingPoints

Staff and parents preparing a Diwali lunch for the school.

Setting the Stage for the Year

Prior to the start of the school year, administrators and teachers made thoughtful decisions about student placements and co-teaching partnerships. Teachers were trained on how to use an Excel spreadsheet to use the school's most recent data and proficiency levels to make their schedules strategically. We wanted to provide support based on need and minimize the number of daily transitions and disruptions that sometimes occur with our most vulnerable students.

Making Meetings Meaningful

Scheduling meetings can sometimes be challenging, and let's be honest, most of the time teachers have so much going on it's easy to forget appointments that are planned on the fly. Our EL teachers used a shared document to schedule collaboration instead of emailing everyone to check their availability. This allowed all parties to see which time slots were taken and which were available. Next, our EL teachers sent an email confirming the selected time, and in doing so, automatically added the meeting time to a shared calendar. By default, an automatic reminder was also sent to everyone one day prior to the meeting. This small action made a huge impact in coordinating collaboration.

Have you ever showed up to a planned collaboration session only to be met with awkward silence? Where no one had taken the ownership of setting out expectations or drafting a meeting agenda?

grades and behavior. Like any translation tool, though, it is not 100 percent accurate. To make translation easier, we used simple sentences.

We even established monthly parent meetings at sites with high ELL populations. One school with a large Punjabi population introduced Chai and Chat—families were welcomed with a cup of tea (chai) to discuss school-related issues, ask questions, make suggestions, and volunteer to showcase aspects of their backgrounds and cultures. Slowly, our language learners and their families were becoming part of the school culture, and families felt empowered.

Blue Jay (SK)

Sayers

Prince Charles

Name: Michelle Gill

Class: iTELL 2019-2020
Integrating Technology to Enhance Language Learning

October 17, 2019

↕ to divider

Focus of Inquiry connected to student learning. (what *evidence* are we using to make decisions)	TBD
Digital Platform	Book Creator

Intended Outcomes:	Norms:
To ensure that this meeting time is purposeful. Hone our capacity to identify the needs of our learners. Work together collaboratively as a team. Create plans for next steps.	Be respectful of time. Be open minded and positive. Come prepared. Stay focused/on topic.

Notes:
- Team will meet Oct 18th to finalized their inquiry question and send to Michelle on Thursday Oct 24th by 10:00am
- Team will also decide on the next monthly meeting date for November
- Quick demonstration/discussion of flipgrid and book creator
- Collecting data using exit tickets. Michelle to send team digital template

- Next meeting date November 14th

Shared digital notebook

In order to run a productive meeting, everyone needs to know the goal, the items to be discussed, and what they need to have prepared. Using a digital notebook created with slides, teachers put together an agenda and added any relevant information they wanted to discuss before the meeting. This gave teachers a shared platform for planning and documenting meeting discussions. Once teachers got the hang of adding information using the text box feature, it was easy for them to resize and adjust elements to fit the slide. Using colored tabs made it manageable to sort and organize all meeting notes. Teachers saw the value in creating notebooks with specific sections for each class they were supporting. One of the most unexpected but impactful outcomes was that using the digital notebook gave teachers a window into each other's classrooms. This sparked powerful dialogue and sharing.

Digital Shared Co-Planning

Determining your starting point and non-negotiables is vital. The dynamic of every partnership will be different, and we have to be patient and respect the process. Yes, sitting together with your colleagues and mapping out long-range goals in one marathon session would make it much easier to support students and meet short-term targets in a timely manner. However, this is not the reality in many schools. After teaching for 15 years, I have learned to take baby steps and allow the relationship to evolve with each interaction. Teachers who are establishing relationships need to know how to make the most of the time they have by identifying the lesson content, process, and product. I call these the "lesson essentials." Without this information, you are simply an extra body reacting to student needs instead of an active participant designing the specific scaffolds embedded in the lesson. Below is an example of the essential elements to discuss when you have limited time.

Lesson Essentials

Content
- What are the students supposed to learn?
- Create learning targets using "I can" statements. I can...

Process
- How will they learn the content? Language Functions

Product
- How will they demonstrate their learning?

Created by Michelle Gill, 2017

Creating A Community of Practice.

In order to share information and resources more efficiently, we created a website-based collaboration system; our ELL Sharepoint. This gave all teachers access to current, high impact instructional strategies, webinars, articles, sound assessment ideas, and colleague-created lessons any time they wanted. All resources could be downloaded and edited to meet the specific needs of students. Knowing it was impossible for teachers to attend every professional development session, we continuously uploaded and archived all slideshows for teachers. However, we knew that even if they reviewed the slides, they would be missing the powerful dialogue and sharing among colleagues. To remedy this, we began using a platform called Nearpod to create professional development presentations. We uploaded existing PowerPoints, Google Slides, and PDFs and converted them into interactive presentations. Teachers loved this! They also saw how it would be an effective and engaging tool in their classrooms, and many of them began using features such as polls, quizzes, open-ended questions, and 3D objects in their lessons. Through the virtual field trip option, teachers provided their students with many new experiences and built background knowledge which helped them connect to the content they were learning. They then uploaded these lessons to Google Classroom so students could go back and rewatch them at any time. Teachers could immediately access reports containing classroom and individual performance, which allowed them to digest the information and use the data to prepare for their next collaboration meeting.

HIGH IMPACT STRATEGIES

Three strategies have transformed how ELs are supported in our district. Number one was moving to an online digital form of co-planning. Next was restructuring the way professional development is delivered, and, finally, using platforms such as Book Creator to allow us to reach all students.

Digital Co-Planning Template

Providing a digital co-planning template for teachers—along with thorough training on each section—has proved to be a powerful way to guide teacher teams. We've found that this comprehensive tool has created more opportunities for teacher communication, collaboration, differentiation, and critical thinking. Why? Because this template led teachers to realize that they don't always have to meet face-to-face for purposeful planning to occur! This digital platform has enabled teachers to streamline collaboration and plan more efficiently. The structure is as follows:

Digital Co-Planning Guide. Made with Google Sheets, includes drop-down feature.

Nearpod

I. Meet Face-to-Face: During this time, classroom and EL teachers decided on the lesson focus and the content that would be used to deliver the curriculum. Questions discussed included, "What is the intention of the unit or project?" "What do we want students to be able to do?" and "How will they demonstrate their learning?" During this meeting, teachers also decided on their specific learning targets. These were based on the types of language most used in academic settings: Recount, Explain, Argue, and Discuss (Lundgren, 2015). A shared Google Sheet containing examples of student-friendly "I can" statements can support educators in determining appropriate language tasks. At the end of this meeting, both teachers knew the goals, content material, specific student activities, and success criteria.

II. Plan Individually: At this stage, the EL teachers embedded scaffolds into the lesson on their own. Because teachers were using a shared digital notebook, they could see additions in real time. EL teachers added visuals, adapted materials, and included sentence frames and more for students. For new partnerships, we suggested using the Talk, Read, Talk, Write structure from Nancy Motley (2016) to ensure all language domains were incorporated. We immediately noticed EL teachers were more intentional when scaffolding. For example, one lesson's scaffolding included the following:

- Inserting anchor charts they created
- Attaching audio to text to support students who would have difficulty reading

Co-planned lesson using TRTW structure

Sticky Note Exit Ticket Template

- Using graphic organizers for collaborative annotation of text
- Embedding documents with the target language function, vocabulary, and sentence frames

III. Monitor Student Progress: Throughout the unit, teachers would monitor students' progress to see who understood the concepts and who required more practice and support. A quick way teachers elicited feedback was through exit tickets. Prompts sometimes included the following:

- What is one new thing that you learned today that you didn't know before?
- What is a question you have about today's lesson—something that has left you puzzled?
- One connection I made to the text was...

A shared template allowed teachers to make customized exit tickets using sticky notes. Many used the template not only for exit tickets but also to create individualized scaffolds for students. For example, implementing an idea from *7 Steps to A Language-Rich, Interactive Classroom*

Samples of NearPod
Exit Tickets

Samples of FlipGrid Exit Ticket
videos "What I learned in summer
school..."

(Seidlitz & Perryman, 2021), we gave students language to use instead of simply saying, "I don't know." Other tools we used to make student feedback easier to manage, archive, and share were Nearpod and FlipGrid.

These tools made learning visible and led to more meaningful discussions during collaboration. Classroom practices were being shaped by the most powerful practice of all—conversation.

Revamping Professional Development Delivery (Monthly Meetings, 1-5-15, and Twitter)

Sometimes, professional development (PD) can feel like just one more thing we have to do. We've all experienced that feeling, but I believe that all educators are lifelong learners who value meaningful development. I would often hear other teachers say that they were frustrated with PD sessions that were always filled with the latest buzzwords with no substance. Here's what many teachers had to say:

- They were done with the jargon.
- They were done with ice breakers.
- They were done with presenters reading off of the slides.
- They were done with feeling like their time had been wasted.

I couldn't blame them, so we revamped our PD practices and priorities to include three primary components that made these programs much more valuable for teachers.

I. Monthly Meetings: When we introduced monthly ELL district meetings, I found myself in the position of providing PD to teachers and I finally understood why it sometimes ends up being a one-size-fits-all approach. Planning and implementing the bulk of PD often falls on the shoulders of a handful of district leaders. Meeting everyone's needs can be extremely difficult; however, the benefits of intentionally creating meaningful, relevant, engaging learning opportunities were worth the effort for both staff and students. So that's exactly what we did! We changed the way we delivered professional development at our monthly meetings. We gave teachers voice, choice, and practice. We started by sending all teachers a Google Form asking two questions:

- What areas and specific training sessions do you want to see?
- Are you willing to share some of your effective go-to strategies?

Now we had a starting point. We could ensure teachers' needs were being met while introducing a few strategies of our own. Each month, EL teachers were released for half a day of training. Of the three-hour session, we typically spent the first hour learning one to three new strategies. The second hour, teachers practiced the techniques they had just learned; we called this our practice lab. Teachers appreciated having trial runs before going live with students. The last hour was dedicated to sharing among colleagues. Teachers had indicated that they wanted to know what practical ideas other teachers were using that they could implement in the classroom right away. Typically, we had one or two teachers volunteer to present a website, app, or strategy that was working well in their building and had impacted student learning. These were recorded, turned into video tutorials, and uploaded to our ELL website.

II. 1-5-15: After reading *The Four O'Clock Faculty: A Rogue Guide to Revolutionizing Professional Development* (Czyz, 2017), I decided to create my own version of the 1-5-15. Understanding that teachers are busier than ever, I wanted to leverage technology to help educators maximize the spare minutes they had and make them meaningful. Using Smore.com, I created monthly bulletins laid out in three sections:

1 = PD that takes about 1 minute

5 = PD that takes about 5 minutes

15 = PD that takes about 15 minutes

The 1-5-15 could offer quick notes on relevant educational topics, with links to supporting articles, templates, resources, and videos. My hope was that, whether teachers had 1, 5, or 15 minutes, the content in the bulletin would impact teacher collaboration and student growth. Feedback from our EL teachers determines the themes. For example, these are some of our past themes:

- **Teacher Bias: The Elephant in the Room**
- **Scaffolding and Assessment**
- **Language Is Culture: Culturally Responsive Teaching**

Furthermore, I hoped that the topics shared would spur further conversations with colleagues. The 1-5-15 was more successful than I could have hoped. I began to schedule follow-up PD sessions based on the information sent out in each bulletin. For example, if the 1-5-15 contained information about the Picture Word Inductive Model (Calhoun,1999), which uses pictures to develop language through thinking, listening, speaking, reading, and writing, I would schedule a 45-minute follow-up session after school for teachers who wanted to continue the discussion or see it in action. Professional development was being delivered to educators in a flexible way, and powerful strategies were now making their way to classrooms across the district to improve student learning!

Feedback from the Field:

"This is the greatest !!!!! It's the pro-d format all teachers have been waiting for. Thank you!"

- Amy LeClair, EL Teacher,
  Aberdeen Elementary

"Awesome, Michelle. Great idea! My Early Literacy Support teachers are starting to use the Picture Word Inductive Model in their co-teaching classrooms. It's a great strategy. Thanks for sharing."

- Bonnie Iftody, District Principal

"I LOVE this! Thank you to all the staff at the curriculum department for their dedication and hard work, coming up with ideas to engage teachers in pro-d. I will definitely be using this at my staff meetings, as well as forwarding the bulletins to my staff."

- Christine Jordan, Principal,
  Bradner Elementary

Sample 1-5-15

The 1-5-15 Bulletins are sent to all teachers, administrators, and support staff in our district every month. Our Early Learning department has teamed up with the ELL department to create them together. This has helped reinforce the notion that we are all language teachers working together.

III. Virtual PD (Twitter)

Lastly, we used the power of Twitter to connect our teachers with experts all over the world. Each year, we run two ELL book studies for teachers in our district. We have been very lucky to have those authors participate, engage, and support us. Through FlipGrid and Padlet, teachers in our district had the pleasure of learning directly from Tonya Ward Singer, Andrea Honigsfeld, Heather Parris, Lisa Estrada, and Katie Gardner.

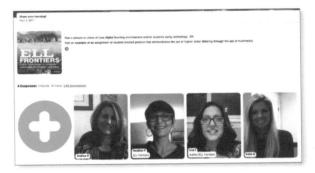

FlipGrid

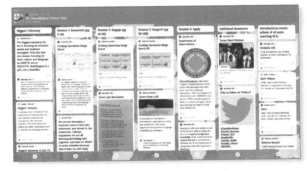

Example of Padlet from EL teacher Book Study

Scaffolding with Book Creator

After exploring many amazing websites, apps, and platforms to introduce to teachers, I finally decided on Book Creator. These were the criteria I used when searching for just the right app:

Simplicity of features.

- Compatibility with iOS and Chrome (the technology available to students and teachers in all of the schools in our district)
- Easy incorporation of the four language functions
- Support for teachers and students as creators
- Opportunities for easy differentiation and collaboration

Book Creator met all of these and so much more! It was an open-ended creation tool that would allow users to develop and publish books. The intuitive platform made it easy to produce interactive pages that combined text, voice, images, audio, and videos. Teachers received two half-day training sessions and weekly school site support. The ELL department purchased licenses for those who were ready to implement this tool into their daily teaching practice, which allowed us to create a number of libraries and add multiple teachers. This enabled both the classroom teachers and the EL teachers to access and comment on student work any time, from anywhere. Teachers began the practice of setting targets and criteria, reviewing student progress, and giving descriptive feedback in a timely manner... *together*.

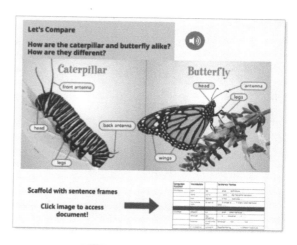

Examples of Scaffolding with Book Creator

As I continued to visit schools weekly, I was able to build capacity by modeling lessons, co-creating templates with teachers, and supporting them during their collaboration meetings. I was able to introduce different ways of utilizing Book Creator in the classroom. During co-planning time, teacher teams were discussing the various ways they could give ELs an entry point into grade-level curriculum without relying on completely different resources. Making material comprehensible was at the forefront during planning. ELs were now being supported throughout the day, even when the EL teacher was not physically in the room.

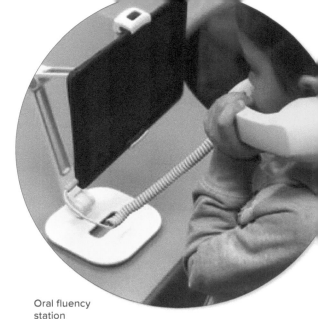

SUCCESS STORIES

Yebeen and Yerin had recently arrived in Canada. They started their grade 4 year just a few months later. Unfortunately, the sisters were placed in different classes.

When Yebeen and Yerin first arrived, teachers took the time to get to know the girls, their likes and dislikes, and their hobbies and other interests. They made note of the girls' assets as well as the areas that needed to be supported. Rather than the EL teacher trying to plan a completely different program to be delivered to the girls in isolation, the two fourth-grade teachers decided to align their term goals and combine their classes for all of the language arts anchor lessons. The anchor lessons focused on the big ideas, such as summarizing a text and finding the supporting details. By aligning their goals and combining their classes, they strategically put themselves in a position to better support all students. Now there were two classroom teachers, one EL teacher, and a learning support service (LSS) teacher present during this block. That meant the ratio of 1 teacher to 24 students shifted to 1 teacher to 12 students.

Using the Daily 5 Framework (Boushey & Moser, 2006), the teachers incorporated technology into literacy stations to enhance their learning tasks. For example, the team created a station that allowed students to record themselves reading in order to practice oral fluency. They then

Oral fluency station

assessed the recordings and added them to each child's digital portfolio. Scannable technology also transformed literacy stations by giving students another way to interact with content. We created QR codes that would connect students to a differentiated text, a website, a YouTube video, or a teacher-created audio clip. We supported teachers in this process by creating a Google Sheet that allowed them to make and share QR codes quickly with students and their co-teachers.

As they planned for the upcoming science fair, the classroom teachers decided that Yebeen and Yerin would have the option of submitting their information in writing instead of presenting orally. To their surprise, the EL teacher shared that the girls wanted to present. Shocked because the only time Yebeen and Yerin spoke in class

Co-planning

Yebeen and Yerin practice videos

Sample Dual-Language Digital Book

was when they were in a small group, the teachers were hesitant but open to this idea. The EL teacher demonstrated how she could use FlipGrid to support the girls even when she wasn't in the building. She shared her knowledge about how this tool allowed teachers to create "grids" that would facilitate video discussions. Each grid was like a message board where students posted videos and teachers could respond and provide timely feedback. It was an engaging way to have students practice their oral language to an authentic audience. Over the next few weeks, the teachers kept track of the girls' progress. They were surprised to see how often the girls were recording—from home! When it came time to present, the girls were confident and truly felt like part of the class.

Both grade-level teachers incorporated a new Daily 5 literacy station that included FlipGrid into the class routine so all students could become competent using this tool. Once word got out about the videos students were creating, all the intermediate students wanted to participate too. Capacity was being built and shared throughout the school, and Yebeen and Yerin became the student leaders for FlipGrid!

The teachers continued to combine classes when they could, not only to lower the teacher-student ratio but because they saw the value in collaborating and sharing ideas. They also learned the power of giving every student a voice.

Dual Language Digital Books

As I was visiting an elementary school, I overheard a voice say, "I don't want anyone to know I speak Punjabi." I know from personal experience that many of our ELs feel like they live in two worlds: one where they embrace and are proud of their culture and one where they feel they need to hide it. So, my colleague and I decided to embark on a project that would link an elementary school with a middle school to enhance students' literacy development while honoring their cultures. Middle school students who were proficient in more than one language would create digital dual-language books to share with elementary schools across the district. All teachers would be able to access the books through our ELL website. The initiative had three main goals:

- To help students see themselves in their classroom and curriculum
- To help students develop a positive sense of self
- To show students that their relationships and cultural contexts help shape who they are

We created a library using Book Creator and shared it with all teachers and students involved. Students wrote and recorded simple text for beginner readers. They recorded in both English and their native languages, which included Punjabi, Spanish, Italian, and Hindi. Students were engaged while developing their academic and linguistic competence in English, and collaboration among students flourished. For example, they had to negotiate word choice when translating because there was not always the exact translation in every language. They often used Google Translate and found synonyms that would work. They also gave careful consideration to sentence structure and what images would match their text. When the elementary students listened to the books and heard their own languages, they connected to the stories on a much deeper level.

Teachers planned to continue using this platform to support students' academic, linguistic, and cultural development. By starting with sound pedagogy, integrating appropriate digital tools, and designing projects that encouraged students to use their native languages, we communicated that we value their cultures and identities.

● ● ● CONCLUSION

Educators (educational assistants, teachers, coaches, principals, vice-principals, etc.) at every school are part of the solution to improving student instruction. We all come with a powerful range of expertise that will help maintain high-level learning for everyone. To be a truly effective team and maximize the strengths of every individual, we need to have shared vision, agency, and ownership. The most effective way to drive change is through collaborative professional development. More than ever, we need to move beyond just the test scores to determine our success. We need to think about the goals that are hard to measure but are the foundation of effective instruction, such as equitable engagement, student belonging, and parent connection. The proper use of technology in the classroom can help teachers differentiate to meet all students' needs. It can also help all ELs share their voice to demonstrate their learning and build a bridge between school and home. It opens the door to powerful teacher collaboration. As you continue this journey, keep in mind, "Learning involves patience and time" (First Nations Education Steering Committee, 2015).

"Change is hard. The first peoples' principles of learning encompass powerful educational perspectives for both aboriginal and non-aboriginal learners. One principle continues to guide me as i support teachers: **'learning involves patience and time.'**"

—MICHELLE GILL

References and Further Resources

Aguilar, E. (2013). *The art of coaching: Effective strategies for school transformation.* Jossey-Bass.

Boushey, G., & Moser, J. (2006). *The daily 5: Fostering literacy independence in the elementary grades.* Stenhouse.

Calhoun, E. F. (1999). *Teaching beginning reading and writing with the Picture Word Inductive Model.* ASCD.

Czyz, R. (2017). *The four o'clock faculty: A rogue guide to revolutionizing professional development.* Dave Burgess Consulting.

First Nations Education Steering Committee. (2015). *First peoples' principles of learning.* http://www.fnesc.ca/first-peoples-principles-of-learning/

Gottlieb, M. (2013). *Essential actions: A handbook for implementing WIDA's framework for English language development standards.* WIDA.

Honigsfeld, A., & Dove, M. G. (2010). *Collaboration and co-teaching: Strategies for English learners.* Corwin.

Motley, N. (2016). *Talk read talk write: A practical routine for learning in all content areas (K-12).* Seidlitz Education.

Lundgren, C. (2015). *WIDA: Introducing the key uses of academic language* [SlideShare] Minnesota English Learner Education Conference. http://www.slideshare.net/MELEdConference/wida-introducing-the-key-uses-of-academic-language

Seidlitz, J., & Perryman, B. (2021). *7 Steps to a language-rich interactive classroom* (2nd ed.). Seidlitz Education.

7

Relationship Building

TENDING TO A SHARED PLOT OF LAND

Sarah Bouwer
and **Tan Huynh**

> "Coming together is a beginning; keeping together is progress; working together is success."
>
> - Henry Ford

SNAPSHOT

There's a difference between surviving and thriving in a partnership. When two educators come together to work toward a common goal, they are most successful when they are able to thrive. Throughout this chapter, we will be sharing our story and the lessons we have learned regarding the importance of relationship building, particularly in the context of collaboration and co-teaching. We share our experiences hoping that what we have learned can help you thrive in your own classrooms and partnerships.

We are both experienced international teachers, having taught for a combined 32 years. Prior to working together, Tan was an English as an Additional Language (EAL) teacher in an international school in Laos, and Sarah was working as an outdoor educator* in China. As part of the same cohort, we joined Saigon South International School in Ho Chi Minh City, Vietnam the same year. This school is an independent, private, international school with students from early childhood to grade 12. It offers advanced placement courses and the International Baccalaureate Diploma Program. We were hired as part of the elementary division, whose philosophy centers around inquiry-based learning. Sarah is one of five homeroom teachers for grade 5. Tan is the designated EAL teacher assigned to support the identified language learners and non-ELs alike. The majority of the student body are multilingual learners for whom English is not the home language.

* Outdoor education focuses on experiential learning: increasing active participation, enhancing problem solving skills, developing social skills, and promoting reflection on classroom experiences.

SETTING THE STAGE

Both of us have lived and worked internationally for many years. Prior to arriving at our current school, we did not know each other. Tan's position was newly created for the grade level. Since his job and the expectations for his work were not clearly articulated, it was left up to each team member to determine how best to work with the new EAL position. In order to optimize our teamwork, we have established a collaborative relationship that consists of co-planning and co-teaching. Because of our schedules, we can only formally plan together once every two weeks. However, depending on whether it is week A or week B, Tan can provide in-class support up to three times a week. With each visit, we can co-teach for up to 70 minutes.

Over our two years of collaboration, we have mapped out units of study at the 30,000-foot level, co-planned and co-taught lessons, created heterogeneous groupings to provide small-group instruction, considered rubrics to use, designed resources and teaching materials, and spent hours conferencing about the needs of individual students. These professional responsibilities are just the tip of the iceberg—the part of our teamwork that other teachers and our administrators see. But what is hidden from view is the tremendous, constant, and subtle work of building trust, sharing our vulnerability, and nurturing our collaborative partnership. Without this interpersonal work, we would never be able to collaborate on behalf of students.

Nurtured: Once trust is earned, team members begin actively seeking each other's support, skill sets, and interests to contribute to future projects.

Earned: Team members build trust by supporting each other's goals and projects.

Formed: Individuals are formally assigned to a team, and each member has a defined role on the team.

Figure 1: The phases of building an asset-based, intentional partnership. Developed by Sarah Bouwer and Tan Huynh.

We choose to collaborate every day; it is not just an assignment given to us at the beginning of the school year. Collaboration is a process, not a result.

Relationships do not happen between teaching partners just because the principal or district-level administrators assign them to work with each other. Our experience shows that they are formed, earned, and nurtured by the partners themselves. When we examined the development of our partnership, we noticed that our relationship moved through the following phases:

1. **Formed:** Individuals are formally assigned to a team, and each member has a defined role on the team. We were formally placed on the same fifth-grade team, and each of us had a specific role. We created a schedule for collaboration that included co-planning and co-teaching.

2. **Earned:** Team members build trust by supporting each other's goals and projects. We added to, and never took away from, each person's ideas and contributions. We always found a way to support each other.

3. **Nurtured:** Once trust is earned, team members begin actively seeking each other's support, skill sets, and interests to contribute to future projects. We took every opportunity to praise each other, celebrate wins, share each other's work with other teachers, and sympathize with each other's concerns. We engaged in informal conversations about life outside of school.

BLUEPRINT

Understand Unit Goals to Create Assessments

Both of us have been in situations that required collaboration, both inside and outside the classroom. We have seen partnerships that have faltered and existed only in survival mode. But we've also seen that the best collaborations and partnerships have many commonalities, whether you're working on a small team or larger teams made up of multiple stakeholders. As we dug deeper and reflected on the past and current partnerships that have worked, we identified three common characteristics. These traits are what allowed our individual partnerships to thrive in the past, and consequently, they're what we have sought to nurture in our present one. These are the core traits we work to develop and nurture:

1. **Attentive Listening:** The health of a relationship is directly linked to the quality of attention we give to our partner.

2. **Intentionality:** Being intentional creates and maintains a positive relationship. Nurturing the relationship is a professional responsibility that directly affects student learning.

3. **Vulnerability and Trust:** To be vulnerable is to trust that the other person will receive you in a positive light and help you develop in areas where you need support.

A relationship is like a shared plot of land that holds great potential. To fully appreciate what the acreage can offer, it cannot be tended to by just one person. Rather, team members need to come to the field with the intention of planting and cultivating the land so that it can become a garden. The first part of readying the shared land is tilling the soil. In a relationship, this means building personal rapport, which lays the foundation of professional relationships.

In Asia, we often look out across the rice fields and admire the beauty and gentle sway of the green rice stalks. Rarely do we think about the hours that the farmers spent bent over, planting, watering, and thinning out the fields. In a similar way, when we think of dynamic teaching relationships, we rarely see the groundwork of active listening, intentionality, vulnerability, and trust. Both of us lay this foundation through our positive daily interactions, and it is the first step in moving from collaboration as an assignment to collaboration as a culture.

Attentive Listening

When building rapport in a relationship, active listening is an essential tool. We have found that body language is like a bullhorn: it can communicate more clearly and loudly than words can. Active listening starts with paying attention to the nonverbal communication that takes place.

The more we are able to be attentive listeners, the stronger our foundation becomes. We make a conscious effort to put away technology that might be a barrier and a distraction when listening. However, active listening does not mean being silent the entire time. It means that we intentionally interact in a way that affirms what is being said. We have found that we can do this in several ways:

- Showing affection by being caring and gentle
- Being humorous (laughing and making jokes when appropriate)
- Validating each other's experiences and feelings
- Being enthusiastic about ideas and suggestions
- Storing our devices as we listen to each other

By taking time to actively listen to one another, we seek to learn from and understand each other. Often we encounter perspectives that are different from what we might have otherwise considered. We provide space for each other to offer our own ideas, but that comes after we have listened fully and attentively to our partner.

From Tan —

During a conversation, I sensed Sarah's enthusiasm as she shared about her students' work regarding the UN Sustainable Development Goals. As she pulled up her laptop, I could hear the eagerness in her voice as she introduced Kiva (www.kiva.org), a microfinancing organization. She was excited to share that her classes in the past had created business plans and voted to implement one of them to raise funds for microloans. I embraced her energy, as I knew this was something she valued and was part of her expertise. Passion should be met with celebration. Therefore, I was excited for her and knew her students would benefit from this experience.

Intentionality

Our definition of intentionality is about valuing the connection, not just the finished outcome, that both of us are working toward. One way that we intentionally built a foundation of trust was to make it a point to get to know one another personally, not for just what we could offer professionally.

A team of researchers noted that relationships that have more positive interactions tend to be happier than those with fewer positive interactions (Gottman, McCoy, & Coan, 1996). From this, we have surmised that one way to be more intentional in our relationship is to make sure that the bulk of our interactions are positive and affirming rather than critical and destructive. Figure 2 offers examples of positive and negative interactions based on Bonner's (2019) concept of relationship banks.

From Sarah —

I grew up in a military family, and as a result, relationships are very important to me. I know that our time together in the international world is probably limited to a few years, and I wanted to make sure that Tan knew I valued this period of working together. Since both of us arrive at school early, I would make a point to stop by his classroom to say good morning and have a quick chat. Often these chats were not related to school, but rather about how we are doing personally. As we were both new to Ho Chi Minh City, I would share places I had explored over the weekend, and Tan would share about movies he'd seen. I was intentional about having these conversations, as I wanted Tan to know that I valued him for who he was, not just because he was a colleague whom I had been assigned to.

SITUATIONS	POSITIVE INTERACTIONS	NEGATIVE INTERACTIONS
Co-Planning Situations	-Build on existing ideas (e.g., *Yes, I also thought about...*) -Present strategies as potential options (e.g., *That's a great idea. We could also try...or...*)	-Completely dismiss existing ideas (e.g., *No. I don't think that would work.*) -Insist on an approach (e.g., *At my previous school, we always...*)
Co-Teaching Situations	-Reinforce our colleague's idea (e.g., *Just like what Mr. Huynh showed you.*) -Praise each other in front of students (e.g., *Thank you, Ms. Bouwer, for...*)	-Contradict a teacher's idea (e.g., *Even though your teacher thinks this way, I think...*) -Correct a teacher in front of students (e.g., *No, that's not correct. It should be done this way...*)
Informal Situations	-Engage in small talk (e.g., weekend, holidays, family) -Connect to our hobbies or interests (e.g., *I saw this article and thought you might like...*)	-Engage in only school-related conversations (e.g., *Can we start the meeting instead of wasting our time with a round-table share of how we are doing?*) -Using judgmental language (e.g., *I wouldn't do that like you did...*)

Figure 2: Positive and Negative Forms of Interactions. Developed by Sarah Bouwer and Tan Huynh.

Vulnerability and Trust

By engaging in difficult conversations, we intentionally invite in vulnerability and its sidekick, trust. In *The Gifts of Imperfection*, Brené Brown (2010) says, "Staying vulnerable is a risk we have to take if we want to experience connection" (p. 53). Vulnerability requires putting yourself out there and being completely open with another person. Since we both intentionally tried to lay a solid foundation for our relationship, we felt safe sharing concerns, hopes, and inner thoughts. We became more transparent as we worked together. As a result, the seed of trust was planted and nourished, and it soon began to grow.

In our collaborative relationship, trust and vulnerability go hand in hand and are the lifelines for a successful partnership. In a recent study about employee engagement, researchers concluded that a lack of clarity bred distrust and disengagement. As engagement eroded, connection and empathy toward one another diminished as well (Brown, 2018b). By establishing intentionality and creating a feeling of safety within our partnership, we made every effort to create room for vulnerability. Because we were clear about our intentions and desired outcomes for our partnership, trust was actively nourished, which led to high engagement when we collaborated.

During our second unit, we wanted to bring in Sarah's international development background to enhance the existing curriculum. However, there was concern that bringing in additional material to strengthen a unit of study might be perceived by others as devaluing the work that had previously been done, which was not the intent. Because trust had been established, it was easier to be vulnerable with each other about the concerns we had. We knew that there would be no personal judgment, and as a result, it was safe to take the risk of being authentic. Returning to the plot of land analogy, vulnerability and trust are the seedlings that have sprouted when the seeds of active listening and intentionality have been sown.

In our collaborative relationship, trust and vulnerability go hand-in-hand and are lifelines for a successful partnership.

HIGH IMPACT STRATEGIES

Provide a Variety of Assessments

If you were to observe us co-planning, you would see how supportive we are of each other's ideas and how affirming we are of each other's strengths. What you would observe is the fruit of our real work: the commitment to fostering a positive relationship with each other. We have three strategies to offer to you: (a) understanding each other's values, (b) identifying and building on each other's strengths, and (c) taking an affirming approach.

A. Understanding Each Other's Values

Education is a field that encompasses various perspectives, philosophies, and beliefs. As actions are rooted in beliefs, it is important to take the time to identify and understand what our colleagues value. Only then can we discern their priorities and motivations. By intentionally leaning into conversations with one another about what each partner sees as important, we affirm that we are curious about the other person and want to better understand them. This allows us to go deeper into our collaboration because we have taken the time to unpack the assumptions we may hold that often hinder effective teamwork. Furthermore, recognizing each other's values allows us to know how to support and build each other up. This skill is rooted in the following practices:

- Actively listening to values that are repeatedly brought up
- Engaging in intentional conversations about educational practices
- Paying attention to one another's practices

Next, we can look for ways to encourage and support one another. When we collaborate, we try to keep what each person holds dear in the forefront. After two years of working together, Tan realized that Sarah values having students make conceptual connections to the unit through her various read-alouds, videos, and novels. When Tan co-teaches with Sarah, he takes every opportunity to have students connect the text to the central concepts of the unit. Sarah appreciates this because she values the higher-order thinking that then occurs.

B. Identifying and Building Upon Each Other's Professional Strengths

When we work together, we get to see what each other brings to the table. In our grade-level team, each teacher has different strengths. For example, we rely on Sarah's extensive social studies and outdoor adventure experience when unit planning. She helps us look for ways to think about social studies content and opportunities to learn experientially. Tan is known as the technology person on the team. When the school offered virtual school due to the COVID-19 pandemic, the team depended on Tan's ability to identify appropriate apps and programs to facilitate online learning. Though Sarah and the other four grade-five teachers have their own classes, what Sarah shares in terms of social studies and outdoor education and what Tan shares related to technology integration benefits all the students in grade five.

We see these strengths as coming from one of two categories: pedagogical expertise and inherent skills. The first is our professional educational background: training, certifications, and teaching strategies. When it comes to a successful partnership, we have to be willing to tap into our colleagues' expertise. Some of the greatest professional resources we have are the people in the room next to us. Imagine what we could learn if we walked across the hall and into the next class. To identify and share these strengths, we have to be amenable to learning about each other and be intentional about making time to collaborate.

When we are receptive to maximizing each other's strengths, we can draw from our toolboxes of strategies to make learning possible, and in the process, we can acquire new strategies and practices from each other. In turn, this process supports our development of new principles and philosophies of teaching. Similar to our students, we thrive when we feel connected to the school community. Taking the time to identify each partner's professional expertise even has a positive impact

upon our students and allows for greater group success. For example, our fifth-grade team relies on Sarah's extensive social studies and experiential learning experience to plan the social studies aspect of our units. Before joining the team, Sarah worked as a middle school social studies teacher, and before that, she spent a few years as an experiential learning facilitator. With her personal expertise, she has brought in knowledge of key concepts such as the five factors of poverty, poverty simulations, and resources to help us create our global poverty unit.

The second category is made up of our inherent skills: personal talents, interests, and passions we are able to showcase through our teaching. In the same affirming way that we see our students for who they are, we need to see our colleagues through the same compassionate eyes and recognize these as personal strengths. When we are able to maximize our personal strengths, we are often able to move into a state of flow. In an interview, Mihaly Csikszentmihalyi defined flow as, "Being completely involved in an activity for its own sake. The ego falls away...Your whole being is involved, and you're using your skills to the utmost" (as cited in Geirland, 1996, p. 2). As colleagues, when we are able to learn from one another and utilize our skills, we are able to move into the state of flow, which in turn has a great impact on student learning.

- Having a growth mindset: We can learn from those around us, so be open-minded and look for the good.

- Finding time: Time is limited; however, how we use our time is what we value.

- Utilizing each other's strengths: Verbalize the strengths you see in your partner, and collaborate to capitalize on each other's talents to be more effective with students.

C. Taking an Affirming Approach

Over our two years of collaboration, we have learned that taking an affirming approach is one of the most effective ways to foster a positive relationship. We both hold strong beliefs about literacy and practice. Some of these beliefs overlap, while others do not. For example, independent daily reading became a contentious topic. One of us believed it was an essential part of literacy development while the other thought that direct instruction through a novel study was the better approach. We had a heated discussion that left us feeling more distant and closed off. Because we wanted to maintain a positive relationship, we talked to each other about the incident and processed what happened the following day.

To give an example, Sarah relies on Tan's personal skills with small-group instruction. Here, Tan is particularly adept at making a concept more comprehensible and helping students transfer thought to writing. As a result, all students are successful in accessing content and producing quality work. Throughout the year, there have been many incidents where our students have been surprised and extremely proud of the work they initially thought they would be unable to complete successfully. However, when we work together and tap into each other's strengths, our classroom community is able to thrive. These are the ways we would encourage others to identify strengths and build a robust partnership:

We learned from this experience that when we have differences in practices and philosophies, we must take an affirming approach. This does not mean that we change our beliefs or practice; rather, it means recognizing that each of us sees literacy development from a different point of view. When we work in each other's rooms, we recognize that literacy development will look different, and we work within those parameters. We also learned that an affirming approach means that we can disagree and still hold our philosophies and practices without being critical and judgmental or using harsh words. A judgment-free partnership means the following things:

- Knowing it is okay to fail, to not know, and to take risks together
- Being real and not feeling like we have to know all the answers
- Being comfortable with not being sure
- Using non-evaluative language with one another
- Affirming each other

Just as Brené Brown (2018a) cautions her readers to avoid using "othering" language—language that separates and categorizes people—we also are aware of the way language can strain a teaching partnership. We have learned to be careful not to use evaluative language during co-planning sessions because one of us may perceive it as a critique. We intentionally use phrases like "What if…" and, "In addition to that idea, we can also…" while avoiding phrases such as "A better idea would be…" or "To make it more effective, you should…" For us to have a successful partnership, we both need to feel safe and be recognized as equal designers of instruction; there is no one "real" teacher and one instructional aide. While co-planning, we make it a point to ask for each other's opinion instead of making executive decisions or assigning roles.

From Tan —

I struggled with using affirming language when I first started collaborating, and I tended to turn co-planning meetings into one-way evaluation sessions. I am embarrassed to confess that I have said things to my colleagues such as, "Let's improve on this part of the lesson" or "How can we make this activity less boring?" My colleagues immediately felt this harsh, judgmental language, and they justifiably became more resistant to collaborating with me. Now, my practice when collaborating with teachers is to use more affirming language such as, "In addition to the lecture, can we offer a visual word bank to facilitate comprehension of the content?" or "Since you want students to learn about photosynthesis, how would you feel if we allowed students to watch videos about photosynthesis in their home language?" This humanizing approach to collaborative conversations encourages my colleagues to lower their barriers to working with me.

All parties in co-planning and co-teaching want and need to feel like competent and capable professionals. Therefore, be mindful of the language used to ensure that everyone's psychological needs are met. This does not mean that we approve or support what we believe are ineffective teaching practices or philosophies. It simply means that we can communicate from a place of compassion and help one another feel a sense of belonging in the partnership, even if there are opposing perspectives.

Every interaction is either a withdrawal or a deposit into the relationship. With each exchange, we can step closer to building a dynamic, collaborative relationship with our co-teacher. Michael Bonner (2019) reminds us that "we cannot withdraw from a relationship we haven't deposited in."

SUCCESS STORIES

Building on a [Story] Plot Together - as told by Tan

As we were co-planning our next lessons during the narrative writing unit, Sarah said she wanted to have differentiated groups for instruction. She had already taught students the basics of the story plot but noticed some students were struggling with the idea of mini-events that built on each other and led to the climax in the story. Therefore, she asked if I could reinforce the concept of a story arc the next day with students who had not fully grasped the concept yet while she worked with those who had.

That day, I noticed how Sarah had printed out all the pages of a read-aloud book and pinned them up under labels for each part of the story arc. When I saw this, I thought it would be a fantastic visual scaffold for me to build on to help students understand the concept of plot (See Figure 3 and 4 below). Although Sarah had prepared a suggested lesson plan, I knew that she trusted my expertise to modify the lesson as needed. Since we had taken the time to co-plan, I understood the outcome we both desired and was able to easily build on what she had already taught.

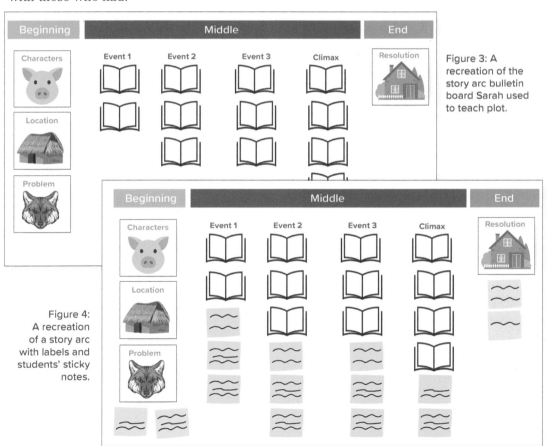

Figure 3: A recreation of the story arc bulletin board Sarah used to teach plot.

Figure 4: A recreation of a story arc with labels and students' sticky notes.

Then the next day, during my lesson with the small group, I instructed students to write out each part of their own stories using sticky notes. The main character was written on one sticky note, the setting would be on another, the first mini-problem was written on yet another, and so forth. After students completed this task, I had them pin their sticky notes under each part of the story arc for their read-aloud. You could see the light bulbs going off as students pinned their sticky notes onto the board. They started realizing the parts of the story arc they had and the ones they were missing (See Figure 3). As a result, they could see where to go back in order to to add the missing sections.

If Sarah and I did not intentionally foster a positive, affirming relationship, this successful collaboration would not have occurred. We trust in each other's professional abilities, so we are comfortable differentiating instruction based on what students need. Because we trust each other's professional judgment, we are both at liberty to adjust the lesson without fear of judgment or misunderstanding. Since I knew what Sarah valued, I built on her previous lesson, which allowed me to tap into the students' prior knowledge. As a result, students were more successful in identifying the areas they needed to improve on for their writing. In this example, we shared the same plot of land, and we both contributed our own tools and skills to build toward student success.

Going back to our garden plot analogy, both of us were tending to the same rice field. Seeds had been sown—in this case,

the background knowledge of plot development. Throughout the unit, each of us used our specific strengths to help foster the students' understanding. Sarah was able to frontload and teach the big picture concepts, while I was able to come in and use my strengths of breaking ideas down for those students who needed additional support. By supporting students and building on the skills we each had, our strategies enabled students to take their narratives, which lacked mini-events that built to a climax, and write an engaging story that they would be proud to share.

Playing to Each Other's Strengths - as told by Sarah

For our first unit, we planned a novel study using the book *Island of the Blue Dolphins*. We focused on inferring types of conflicts that characters encountered and identifying the various actions they might take to resolve each conflict (See figure 5). Although most students identified the conflict and solution, a small group of students struggled to pinpoint the solution to the conflict as it had to be inferred based on textual evidence.

Because Tan and I have a strong, established relationship, we will informally pop into each other's rooms to talk about upcoming plans. One morning, I dropped into Tan's room and shared a few of the trends that I was seeing with students. I shared a graphic organizer I had created that the students had worked on during class. I then asked Tan if he would be willing to provide small-group instruction

TYPE OF CONFLICT	WHAT THE "CONFLICT" WAS - PAGE #	WAS THERE A SOLUTION? IF SO, WHAT WAS IT?
Person against person	The Aluets tell Chief Chowig to give them their fish however, Chief Chowig refuses to give them the fish. - pg 8 ✓	The Aluets asked to give them the fish, however Chief Chowig refused. They said they'd tell Cap't Orlov, but Chief Chowig still wouldn't give it to them. ✓ *Teacher note: So they "solved" the problem by threatening the Chief.*
Person against self	The conflict was between Cap't Orlov and himself- to give Chief Chowig the beads or not. - pg 11 ✓	Cap't Orlov didn't end up giving Chief Chowig the beads, so they ended up having a huge fight. ✓
Person against self	It's the Aluet hunter's choice to shove Chief Chowig or not - pg 12 *Teacher note: It sounds like the conflict in this passage would be that he shoved Chief Chowig.*	The Aluet hunter decided to shove Chief Chowig, so he fell into the rocks and blood was all over his face and he died. ✗
Person against self	Kimki decided to set off alone to the place where he lived in the past. - pg 15 *Teacher note: Why did he do this?*	He decided to leave the island to find a better place for his people to move to.
Person against person	Chief Chowig didn't agree with Karana. Karana told him to stop the hunters, however he didn't agree with her. - pg 9	Chief Chowig didn't agree with her, so he allowed the Aluets to kill the otters to trade for the beads.
Person against nature	The weather is cold, so the fish don't come up to land because it's cold. It's really difficult to fish during this time. - pg 7 ✓	The people in San Nichols Island found fish during this time. They were really happy because during this time, fish don't come to land. ✗ *Teacher note: How is this a solution?*

Figure 5: Identifying conflict and solutions. Recreation of student work sample.

to this group of students and reteach the concept. My thought was that perhaps by hearing a different approach and perspective, this group of students might be able to identify the clues in the story to draw their inferences. As usual, Tan was more than happy to support my request.

Based upon our conversation, Tan created a new document to scaffold students' understanding of conflict and perspective. When Tan recreated a graphic organizer for that lesson, he showed me and asked for feedback, emphasizing why he developed certain aspects. We played to each other's strengths and honored how each other works differently. What was important to me was that we collaborated to achieve the same goal of student success. Figure 6 shows how Tan created a new graphic organizer to support the small-group instruction.

After Tan's lesson, the students had a much clearer understanding of how to use the clues within the novel to draw together their inferences. By reinforcing the skills they had learned, this organizer allowed students to practice and apply them in a different context. As their understanding grew, they began to use these techniques independently with their reading.

TEXTUAL EVIDENCE	WHY WAS THIS A CONFLICT?	WHAT WAS THE SOLUTION?
Captain Orlov offered to give Chief Chowig only one part of every three otters caught.		
Karana wanted Chief Chowig to stop the Aleuts from hunting the otters.		
The Aluets wanted Chief Chowig to share the white bass with them.		
The women took over the men's previous responsibilities.		

Figure 6: A graphic organizer Tan created to explicitly teach the inferencing connected to the conflicts.

From Sarah —

For our expository writing unit, I wanted the students to create a non-fiction magazine centered on a global issue they were interested in. To help capture their interest and guide their investigations, I had created mini research cards for students. On each card, I included an overview about the global issue, an open-ended research question, and a mini case study. As I wanted to ensure that the students had a variety of topics to select from, I asked Tan if he would like to develop more cards for topics the students might be interested in. Together we identified topics, guiding questions, and case studies that were age-appropriate. For consistency, Tan used a sample card that I gave him as his template.

From Tan —

When Sarah initially approached me about helping her create the research cards, I was a little hesitant as I had never created these before. I knew I would be challenged because I lacked the background content knowledge that Sarah wanted on each card. However, I was willing to be open-minded and receptive to taking risks because I knew that by helping to prepare these cards, I could help ensure the students would be more successful with the research project that she had in mind.

Sarah was encouraging and positive throughout the process. When she had to explain the concept or context, I never felt belittled or inferior for not having her depth of content knowledge. As we often play to one another's strengths, Sarah relied on my ability to make academic content accessible to language learners just as I relied on her content expertise. As I showed Sarah my work, I felt affirmed that not only was I being challenged in something new, but I was able to do work that was outside of my comfort zone. If she had been judgmental in her evaluation of my work, I would have been discouraged and more hesitant to collaborate with her in the future.

EAL teachers are highly skilled educators who can be counted on to provide instruction for students. It takes a proactive and open-minded general education teacher to dynamically integrate the language specialist into class lessons. We encourage EAL teachers to always be flexible, adaptive, and responsive to the recommendations of general education teachers. We also urge grade-level and content-area teachers to actively listen to EAL teachers' suggestions, ideas, and approaches to learning. When teachers accept every opportunity to support one another, they can grow and nurture collegial relationships. Each one of us is 50 percent of a partnership, but we all have to walk through 100 percent of the doors opened to us if we want to build trust and rapport.

By co-planning and working together, we were able to maintain high expectations for all students, ensuring that our language learners were exposed to the same content and expected to do the same level of thinking as non-ELs. As this was the first extended research paper they would write for grade 5, we knew that such large global topics could be daunting. The students needed content that was accessible to their reading levels and help identifying global issues they would find interesting and connect to. We wanted the students to know that creating a magazine from high-quality research was something everyone could do successfully.

When students selected their research cards, they were both intrigued and eager to jump into the research process. That enthusiasm for research and a quality writing product was the goal we hoped for. Within days, students were carrying around their cards and eagerly sharing with one another the research they had found about their topic. As a result, the enthusiasm the students had for their topics continued throughout the research process, and their final magazines were ones they were proud to share, not just with their classmates but with others outside the classroom as well.

●●● CONCLUSION

No partnership is problem free. Tuckman's (1965) classic four-part process for group collaboration—forming, storming, norming, and performing—includes a stage for stress overload. Storming is a phase when individuals disagree and experience conflicts as they begin to collaborate. In our teaching careers, both of us have experienced teams that were highly challenged in moving out of the storming stage. Thankfully, we did not encounter this phase in our teaching partnership.

Taking lessons that we had learned into account, we made it our practice to intentionally approach our partnership through the lens of asset-based collaboration. As a result, we rarely have conflicts when we collaborate, which we recognize is an anomaly. Many teachers come to school with a team already formed for them. However, we believe that no matter how a partnership starts, we can begin to earn the trust and respect of our colleagues by actively listening, being intent on having affirming interactions, and being vulnerable. By being mindful of using respectful, judgment-free language and by recognizing each other's values and strengths, we begin to nurture each other, which fosters a sense of community and a desire to continue to collaborate.

We hope that teachers do not have to experience storms before they can form working relationships. The strength of our relationship is the result of our intentions to build one. The relationship we have is the fruit of our actions. Therefore, even when teachers cannot choose the people on their teams, they can still choose to act in ways that create the conditions for positive partnerships. Our students will reap the reward when teachers unite and combine forces. Tan likes to say, "When adults can't play nice, students pay the greatest price."

If you find you and your colleagues are assigned to tend to the same plot of land, we encourage you to roll up your sleeves and begin building a positive, dynamic, long-lasting teaching relationship by planting seed by seed. At the end of the year, you will look back and marvel at the garden that is now ready for harvesting.

References and Further Resources

Bonner, M. (2019, June 23-26). *By design*. [Conference presentation]. ISTE 2019 Conference, Philadelphia, PA, United States. https://conference.iste.org/2019/program/search/detail_presenter.php?id=112419646

Brown, B. (2010). *The gifts of imperfection: Let go of who you think you're supposed to be and embrace who you are*. Hazelden.

Brown, B. (2018). *Dare to lead: Brave work. Tough conversations. Whole hearts*. Random House.

Brown, B. (2018, May 17). *Dehumanizing always starts with language*. https://brenebrown.com/blog/2018/05/17/dehumanizing-always-starts-with-language/.

Geirland, J. (1996, September 1). *Go with the flow*. WIRED. https://www.wired.com/1996/09/czik/

Gottman, J. M., McCoy K., & Coan, J. (1996). The specific affect coding system. In J. M. Gottman (Ed.), *What predicts divorce: The relationship between marital processes and marital outcomes* (Kindle location 1567-1732). Erlbaum.

Tuckman, B. (1965). Developmental sequence in small groups. *Psychological Bulletin*, *63*(6), 384–399. https://doi.org/10.1037/h0022100

8

Cultivating
Collaborative Practices
WITH RELUCTANT
TEACHERS

Valentina Gonzalez

SNAPSHOT

My work in education goes back over two decades. I entered my first classroom as a third-grade language arts teacher mid-year in 1997, in a suburban district outside of Houston, Texas. As a general education classroom teacher, I always taught language arts and social studies and had English learners (ELs) among my students. After many years of teaching in a general education setting, my love for languages and my own personal immigration story led me into a new role as an English as a second language (ESL) instructional support specialty teacher. This meant that I had the privilege of working closely with classroom teachers to provide high-quality instruction that was comprehensible for the growing population of ELs we served. In addition, I worked in small groups with newcomer students to give them accelerated English language development lessons. The model of instruction was both in-class support and pull-out. The chapter that follows chronicles experiences to cultivate collaborative practices with reluctant teachers from my years both in the general education classroom and as an ESL in-class support teacher.

SETTING THE STAGE

"Welcome back everyone!" It was the first faculty meeting of the school year, and my principal stood before us as everyone buzzed around the room, happy to see old friends and eager to meet new ones. "This year, one of our goals is to improve the scores we produce with our English learners. We would like to ask each of you to collaborate with the ESL special programs staff." Suddenly the energy in the room seemed to deflate like a flat tire. I looked around and noticed eyes rolling and heard the faint murmur of whispers. "They can offer planning guidance and model lessons for you to help enhance language development during content instruction." The murmur seemed to grow louder. "Would anyone like to volunteer to have an in-class support teacher in their room for part of the day?" Not. A. Word. Silence. No one spoke up.

It was at this moment that I began to seriously consider why, as a collective group of educators, we are reluctant to open our doors and share our students, our classrooms, and our practices with one another. Why do some teachers shy away from collaboration, close their doors, and work in silos? And how can we change the landscape of teaching so that collaborative practices are embraced as part of the everyday fabric of instruction?

Reluctancy Exists

I remember my first year as a special programs teacher. I had high hopes and aspirations about working with the staff at my campus. I imagined fitting into grade-level plannings and teaching side-by-side with general education teachers. Unfortunately, my imagination and reality didn't always align. Reluctancy to collaborate with other educators exists. It just does. The more I pretended that it didn't, the more I was fooling myself. Recognizing reality was the first step toward progress. Some teachers were not comfortable with collaboration, and I identified several reasons behind their resistance:

- Negative experiences with collaboration in past
- Perceived ideas about collaboration
- Personal work style or personality

I also had to acknowledge that I may never discover why a teacher doesn't initially want to collaborate, but I can still work toward building collaborative practices.

The next step was knowing what to do when I was faced with colleagues who were reluctant about teaming up to enhance instruction. And it became evident that both new teachers and more seasoned teachers could be affected by feelings of opposition to collaboration. This is largely because, traditionally, educators have worked in isolation behind closed doors (Honigsfeld & Dove, 2019). I have seen many classroom teachers come to work daily, walk into their classrooms, and promptly close the door. Even I fell victim to this routine one year after being on a team that did not value collaborative practices. We planned our lessons on our own, taught our students, and went home at the end of the day. Teachers who are not accustomed to planning, evaluating, sharing, discussing, observing, and teaching with others may not welcome these professional activities with open arms. In fact, they may push back and show feelings of displeasure.

Are Collaborative Practices for Everyone?

Collaborative practices are not necessarily natural for everyone. As a special programs teacher, I had to realize that collaboration is a two-way street. All stakeholders needed to be ready and willing to work together. It wasn't just about general education teachers and their willingness to collaborate; it was also about me. I had to learn to be flexible, to listen more, and to assume that no matter what, we all had students' best interest at heart. For some, being comfortable and happy with collaboration takes more time than for others. Working with a team or a partner takes greater intention, and it may even take purposeful planning.

But are collaborative practices for everyone? The simple answer is yes. They are for everyone, but not everyone will collaborate the same way. And the ease with which we find a rhythm in our collaborations will vary. One group of

collaborating teachers explained that they worked with a special programs teacher who wasn't interested in sharing, planning together, or socializing. No matter how much they tried, this teacher just wasn't having it. Very rarely have I encountered teachers like this one, but it does happen. We came to realize that this teacher's own social behaviors and style strongly affected the way he interacted with his colleagues. Though he was excellent with students and extremely knowledgeable in his field, he struggled with building relationships with his colleagues. The key was understanding who he was, respecting his boundaries, and honoring his strengths. Once they recognized his strengths, they were able to slowly build on those, using them as leverage toward collaboration, celebrating small successes along the way.

The Many Faces of Collaborative Practices

There's not one singular way to think of collaborative practices. Co-teaching, in-class support, teaming together to lesson plan weekly, long-range curriculum mapping, co-creating assignments, co-evaluating assessments, teaming up to conduct parent-teacher conferences, attending professional development opportunities as a team, and co-designing literacy nights, field trips, etc. are all forms of collaborative practice (Honigsfeld & Dove, 2019). Knowing that there were many entry points and avenues for collaborative practices helped me a few times when confronted with reluctant colleagues. One teacher, who was very much against collaborating on lesson plans, was happy to invite me to parent-teacher conferences. This was my way in, and I eagerly took it! As I gained her trust and we began to bond, she slowly began to invite me into her instructional world. We began to discuss upcoming units. When she shared that she was about to begin a unit on the Texas Revolution, I asked if she needed any visuals or sentence stems, and she accepted. I noticed that she liked the visuals I gave her and that they were up in the room, labeled with the sentence stems underneath. I knew they were a hit when she asked me for visuals and sentence stems for the unit following the Texas Revolution. This was a big win and the beginning of much more collaboration. Ultimately, we came to realize together that the goal of collaborative practices is to enhance instruction for all students.

Not Just One More Thing To Do

Year after year, educators are faced with new initiatives and new programs. Some take hold while others start and then simply disappear. When initiatives come and go, educators can become jaded. In education, no one has time for one more thing to do. But collaborative practices are not initiatives, and they aren't just one more thing to do. On my campus, it was my job to flip the script. I needed my colleagues to see collaborative practices from a different perspective, one that's not new but that reframes what we're already doing. I had to present collaborative practices as a way to reduce workload rather than add to it—to share students, to share planning, to share evaluation, and to share responsibilities.

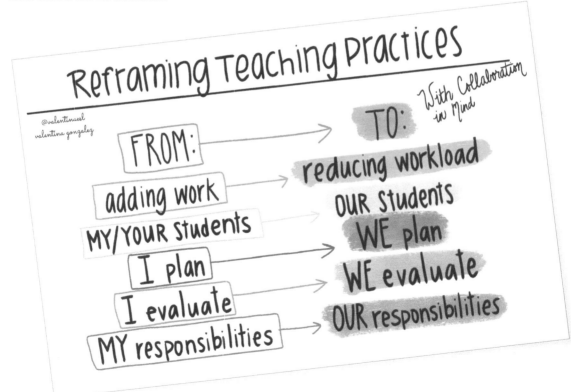

> I needed my colleagues to see collaborative practices from a different perspective, one that's not new but that reframes what we're already doing.

One of my first and most significant experiences with collaborative practices began when I was a general education third-grade language arts teacher. A new student from Venezuela had just arrived, and the ESL special program teacher was assigned to come into my room during language arts to provide support and reduce the student-teacher ratio. This approach was called "in-class support," which meant the ESL teacher would join my classroom for about 45 minutes daily and provide linguistic support. I was excited about this new adventure. Throughout my years as a teacher, I had never had another teacher in my room. It was always just me and occasionally an aide. I'd had ELs in my classroom but not with the support of an additional educator.

As my in-class support teacher worked one-on-one with students or small groups, I eagerly observed the linguistic support she provided. I watched as she modeled the use of sentence stems, visuals, and adapted texts to meet students' needs. Though the model of instruction we had was not a true co-teach approach, we did our best to leverage each other's strengths, plan informally, and teach alongside one another when we could. I never had more work to do because of the ESL teacher in my room; in reality, I had less because there were two of us to spread the work between.

The relationship the ESL teacher and I formed was instrumental in my future experiences with collaborative practices. Through this initial encounter collaborating with another educator to enhance instruction, I learned to plan together, share instructional space, learn from one another, reflect on student progress, and much more. In fact, I'm *still* learning.

It Takes Effort

Don't get me wrong. Not every collaborative experience I had after that was as peachy. No, that's not the case. The fact is that collaboration does take effort on everyone's end. And if you are experiencing a challenge in collaborative practices, you are not alone. I learned along the way that challenges in collaborative practices do not signify that I'm doing something wrong. Instead, I began to see challenges as opportunities to take a step back, analyze the circumstances, and learn about colleagues, students, teaching, and learning.

BLUEPRINT

Serving alongside many educators taught me to approach collaboration systematically. In fact, using the three steps below with any teachers that I collaborate with (not just reluctant teachers) is a proactive approach rather than reactive. The three steps toward cultivating collaborative practices with reluctant teachers include (1) building trusting relationships, (2) learning alongside one another, and (3) being patient with the process. This blueprint will guide you in leveling up collaborative practices with reluctant teachers.

Build Trusting Relationships with Partners

Prolific writer and leader in professional learning and instructional coaching Dr. Jim Knight (2016) says, "When trust exists there is learning, joy, and love. When trust does not exist, there is caution, inertia, and fear" (p. 188). Building trusting relationships is crucial when working with reluctant teachers. A partner who is reluctant to collaborate will rarely be free to share planning, discuss students, and teach together if trust is lacking. To nurture the relationship, I focus on four activities:

- Taking time with one another
- Keeping my word and confidentiality
- Listening to my partner
- Minding the verbal as well as the nonverbal language I use

Professional collaborative relationships take time to build, especially when one party pushes back or isn't on board. Very rarely do professional collaborative relationships happen overnight (or even within the first grading period of school). I've been able to overcome obstacles with partners who were not initially agreeable by remembering that when conflict arises or opposition shows up, it doesn't mean this is the end of the collaboration.

Trust is built bit by bit through many small moments (Brown, 2018). Some teachers are reluctant to collaborate because their trust in colleagues has been broken in the past. One teacher shared with me that she'd rather work alone because she always feels like she's doing more work than her partners. Another described how it felt to be constantly let down by her partner. Knight (2016) describes trust like the air we breathe: "We don't notice when it's there, but when it's gone, everything stops" (p. 204).

When I was an in-class support teacher, my schedule was hectic and changed frequently. There were times that I went into five classrooms daily. I was going from a fifth-grade room to a fourth-grade room and then running back to fifth grade and so on. My colleagues counted on me to be on time and to be where I said I would be. I recognized the importance of trust here because when I was a general

Build trusting relationships with partners.
•
Learn alongside one another.
•
Be patient with the process.

education teacher, I had an ESL special programs teacher who came in to support my classroom. I remember times when they were late or didn't show up at all. I was counting on them, but each time they didn't follow through with their end of the agreement, their reliability decreased, and my trust in them decreased. Slowly, I myself became reluctant to collaborate. Why should I collaborate with someone who isn't all in like I am? Through these experiences, I learned that it was important to show my commitment in several ways:

- Be on time
- Be present
- Bring resources to planning
- Promise only what I could deliver

Another key element of trusting relationships in school is ensuring that each person believes we are in this for the students and not here to judge one another. I've had the pleasure of being on both sides of collaborative practices as a general education teacher and as a special programs teacher. No matter which side I was on, confidentiality was a critical element of cultivating trusting relationships with resistant teachers. As a general education teacher, I wanted to feel confident that when I was collaborating with a colleague, what we said was between us. If I had another teacher in my room, I didn't want to feel that my teaching was being judged. Teaching in front of a colleague is a very vulnerable feeling. I knew that I wasn't a perfect teacher. None of us are, and we all make mistakes teaching. I certainly didn't want my colleagues to share my shortcomings with others. When I became a special programs ESL teacher, I kept

these feelings in the forefront as I went into planning meetings and classrooms. Reluctant teachers will rarely share experiences with colleagues they don't trust, so I made sure to do the following:

- Walk away from gossip
- Keep out of negative conversations
- Share only instructional practices
- Carefully consider what I said and how I spoke about students or teachers

Breaching confidentiality can make it difficult, if not impossible, to create the right circumstances for collaborative practices. I realized that anyone who gave me the privilege to plan or teach with them deserved my confidentiality and that many educators who seem reluctant to collaborate have been burned before and may be healing from past relationships. Trust can quickly be broken, but it takes a great deal of time to repair.

Listening can yield great gains with colleagues who are reluctant about collaborative practices. Think of a time that you have felt you weren't being listened to. When teachers feel they aren't being heard, they may stop sharing. A few years ago, I worked with a team of general education teachers during their weekly planning period. The agreement was that we would each come to the regularly planned time with resources to share on the upcoming units. It was easy to pick up on who were the dominant teachers on the team and who were less confident in sharing. Each time one of the newest teachers tried to share her ideas, the others began to talk and fidget, looking through their folders, and another teacher quickly interrupted to share what they did last year. After a few planning meetings that went this way, the new teacher stopped sharing and sat quietly during meetings.

It's easy to tell when we aren't being listened to. Common indicators include lack of direct eye contact, wandering eyes, fidgeting, interrupting, responding without commenting on what was said, or missing the point. Clearly there is a difference between hearing and listening. What I learned from observing this team's planning meetings is to provide space for each partner to share what they know, believe, and can do. While it may be tempting to interrupt and jump in to share your thoughts, hold back and allow your partner to have the floor (Brown, 2018). Listen without the intent to reply. Rather,

Lesson Planning Tool for Collaborative Teachers

Content Objective (What do students need to know?)
Language Objective (Which language domains will students use to demonstrate learning?)
Evidence of Student Success (How will we know they got it?)
Background Knowledge (What do students already know about this objective?)

Activities (What planned instructional activities or strategies will lead to the objectives?)	Resources/ Materials (What resources & materials do we need?)	Grouping				Assessment (How will we know if students understand? Product, formal, informal, etc.)
		Whole Group	Individual	Partner	Small Group	
1.						
2.						
3.						
4.						

give your partner the space they need to feel respected as the educator they are. Convey body language that indicates listening. Lean in, nod, and hold eye contact. When replying, add to the words your partner spoke. Validate what they said, and contribute to the conversation. If conversations begin to wander off-task or become dominated by one partner, you can implement lesson planning tools during co-planning meetings to help effectively guide and focus the dialogue on the task at hand. The Lesson Planning Tool (see p. 148) is one that collaborative planning partners can use as they plan instruction for classrooms that have English learners. The tool can be used by teachers who co-teach, teachers who work in an in-class support setting, or by those who only plan together.

Additional Academic and Linguistic Considerations

Students who are English Learners	Proficiency Levels in English				Instructional Accommodations	Differentiated Assessment
	Listening	Speaking	Reading	Writing		
1.						
2.						
3.						
4.						
Notes						

Lesson Planning Tool for Collaborative Teachers

Content Objective (What do students need to know?)
Students will be able to retell a story by using words and illustrations.

Language Objective (Which language domains will students use to demonstrate learning?)
Students will retell a story to a partner using language such as: In the beginning...
The setting is...The main characters are...The problem is...First....Then....In the end....The
problem was solved...

Evidence of Student Success (How will we know they got it?)
Students will write a retelling of a story using the paragraph frame: In the beginning...
The problem is...In the end....

Background Knowledge (What do students already know about this objective?)
Students have been exposed to many stories and retellings by the teacher.

Activities (What planned instructional activities or strategies will lead to the objectives?)	Resources/ Materials (What resources & materials do we need?)	Grouping				Assessment (How will we know if students understand? Product, formal, informal, etc.)
		Whole Group	Individual	Partner	Small Group	
1. Students talk about what they did after school yesterday. (TALK)	NA			x		Informal observation (randomly call on a few students to share)
2. Teacher leads the class in reading the BME anchor chart. Focus on identifying what BME is. (READ)	BME anchor chart	x				Informal observation (QSSSA-knowing how to retell is important because...)
3. Students use the sentence stems to retell a book they are reading. (TALK)	Sentence stems				x	Informal observation (listen in on each group- take anecdotal notes-who needs more support?)
4. Students write a paragraph using the frame. (WRITE)	Writer's journals, students' reading books, and paragraph frames		x			Written response in writing journal

Additional Academic and Linguistic Considerations

Students who are English Learners	Proficiency Levels in English				Instructional Accommodations	Differentiated Assessment
	Listening	Speaking	Reading	Writing		
1. Juan	i	i	b	b	Primary language support, bilingual dictionary, visuals	Opportunity to write in primary language, draw and label
2. Renan	i	i	i	i	Primary language support, bilingual dictionary, visuals	Opportunity to verbalize, draw and label in English
3. Li	a	i	h	a	Student exemplars, opportunity to verbalize prior to writing	
4. Victoria	h	h	h	h	Advanced sentence starters	

Notes
During in class support time, work with Juan and Renan to practice retelling using visual sorting cards.
With Li and Victoria, add in theme or lesson.

Learn Alongside One Another

The more focused we are on ourselves, the less trust we gain from partners we hope to collaborate with (Knight, 2016). Learning alongside one another sends the message that we are in this together. We are a team. Resistance to collaboration can grow when teachers feel a hierarchy or competition between one another. As collaborative partners, learning alongside one another demonstrates that neither is superior to the other and that we each bring strengths to the table. Why is this important with teachers who push away from collaboration? There are various ways to learn alongside one another. I love how Staehr Fenner and Snyder (2017) encourage teachers to observe one another with a lens for integrating academic

> **When special programs teachers and general education teachers collaborate to attend professional learning together, both can make many strides. The opportunity offers the pair the chance to build relationships as well as gain new learning as a team.**

language. The years I served as a special programs teacher were the years I grew most as a professional. I learned daily, and from every classroom I went into. My colleagues were my instructors, each one unique in their lesson delivery and classroom management styles. As I traveled from room to room supporting both students and teachers, I picked up new strategies and instructional methods that I would carry to the next classroom and model there. One day I went into a fourth-grade classroom that I supported regularly, and I watched as the general education teacher effortlessly implemented a classroom routine to help students quickly get into the lesson. Students were instantly engaged and participating with their peers. Later that day, when I went to another classroom for in-class support, I tried out the method myself with a small group of students. It worked beautifully. Though being observed by a peer can be a vulnerable experience, it can also lead to great discussions and growth for both parties.

Another way to learn alongside one another is by attending professional learning opportunities as a pair or in teams. A few years ago, I worked in a district that encouraged general education teachers and their collaborative partners to attend a conference for teachers of English learners together. We successfully sent many pairs of co-teachers and teaching partners to the conference, which allowed general education teachers to learn alongside their special programs teachers.

When special programs teachers and general education teachers collaborate to attend professional learning together, both can make many strides. The opportunity offers the pair the chance to build relationships as well as gain new learning as a team. Both educators hear the same message and the same language, yet they each receive it through their own lens of understanding. One year, my co-teaching partner and I discovered a great learning opportunity that was coming to our area. We wanted to go together, so we gathered all the details about it. We shared with our principal that we wanted to attend the conference together to learn new strategies and methods to support our English learners in writing, and we promised to bring back what we learned and share it with our team. We were given the green light, and were grateful to attend together. As a pair, we bounced ideas off one another and discussed how we could implement the methods with the students we had in our classroom. As promised, after the training, we shared what we learned with our team and we continued to incorporate the strategies as we planned together.

Unsure about funding for these opportunities? Some teachers use grant funds for professional learning; others seek funds from their parent teacher association (PTA) or parent teacher organization (PTO).

One more way to learn alongside one another is through modeling lessons. Not only does modeling lessons help to build collaborative practices with reluctant teachers but it also demonstrates strategies that promote language and literacy. I got this started by asking a teacher if I could try out a lesson in her classroom. Once the teacher saw that I was capable of teaching and that the lesson was effective, she asked me to come back regularly. Soon, word got around, and other teachers wanted my collaboration too. I learned along the way that it helped to ask teachers to give me feedback during my lessons. For example, "When I try out this lesson, can you give me feedback on my questioning techniques? I'm trying to ask stronger questions to elicit deeper student discussion." Or, "During this lesson, can you take notes for me on how I redirect students who are off task? That's something I've been working to improve." Giving partners a focus during the lessons enhanced their experience as well as encouraged them to do the same when the roles are reversed. Engaging my colleagues with an active role in observing and giving me feedback also built trust. It sent them a message that I valued and respected their input and that this was teamwork.

Be Patient with the Process

It took me a while to realize that I can't expect collaborative practices to be perfect right away—or ever. Be patient. Working together with one or more teachers takes time. I had to give myself and my colleagues permission to take the time needed to create the type(s) of relationships we desired in order to maximize educational outcomes. Some of the best collaborative practices I have experienced grew over multiple years and through many joint professional experiences.

The problem is that, like many educators, I have a desire to fix things right now. Sometimes I am impatient. I want to solve problems as quickly as I can. That's when I have to remind myself that relationships, change, and challenges take time, and time requires patience. By permitting myself to take time and be patient with collaborative practices, I began to recognize that collaboration is not a race or a competition. We are investing in our students' futures by working together to provide the best educational experiences.

There's a common saying: "How do you eat an elephant?" And the answer is, "One bite at a time." If we think about our approach to collaborative practices as an investment that builds over time rather than one that is made overnight, we will see greater gains.

HIGH IMPACT STRATEGIES

Along the way, I've learned from many educators I've personally collaborated with, as well as from great authors and researchers. Five high impact strategies that I frequently use include (a) plan for success; (b) talk less, listen more; (c) aim for parity; (d) share the spotlight; and (e) promote inclusion. These strategies for collaborative practices with reluctant teachers successfully defuse difficult situations.

Plan for Success

Planning face-to-face at regularly designated times and dates with the grade-level teams and special programs teachers is a best-case scenario. Grade-level teams typically gather weekly at a designated time and day. Each member brings resources, materials, and ideas to share. Attending this type of weekly meeting allows for collaborative practices as teachers plan upcoming lessons. The platform to discuss students' needs and create lessons together is perfect. Regularly scheduled planning meetings between general education teachers and special programs teachers allow for several advantages:

- Opportunities to bond
- Time to build relationships
- Clear paths for communication
- Platforms for all members to be accepted and valued
- Opportunities for special programs teachers to provide scaffolds and accommodations

Honigsfeld and Dove (2019) describe how each member of a collaborative partnership brings value to the experience:

> Teachers with general-education, content-specific expertise offer their knowledge of the subject matter content, general-education curricula, and local, state, and national content-related standards and assessments to all other teachers on staff. At the same time, ELD/ELL specialists have the opportunity to share their expertise in second language acquisition, cross-cultural understandings, bilingualism and biculturalism, and literacy development (p. 35).

Unfortunately, the ability to meet face-to-face with grade-level teachers weekly is rare for special programs teachers who serve multiple grade levels. Many special programs teachers spend the day traveling from one class to the next on very tight schedules. Lack of time to plan together can be a cause of reluctance from general education teachers who work with special programs teachers. Honigsfeld and Dove (2019) caution that, "It is a common occurrence for specialists not to be included as permanent members of interdisciplinary teams: they are generally fewer in number and service students in multiple grades across various disciplines" (p. 136). When special programs teachers are not embraced as valuable members and contributors, they can instead become marginalized and underused.

So what do we do if we are unable to meet regularly in person during a common planning period? Becoming resourceful is the next course of action. In one school where I worked, general education teachers had a "super planning day" every grading period. This was a half-day designated for long-range planning. While general education teachers planned, their students were in the care of special programs teachers and other staff members. The ESL team and I advocated for each of us to have the opportunity to be in the long-range planning meetings with the grade levels we served. It was important for us to be there. We wanted to know what the upcoming units would be so that we could begin pulling materials and resources, and we wanted to support general education teachers with accommodations. Had we not met with the school leadership and let them know how important this was and why, it's likely that we would not have been included in the planning meetings.

Sharing lesson plans electronically works for teachers who are unable to meet face-to-face. Shareable platforms (such as Google Drive or OneDrive) that allow multiple users to collaborate on documents simultaneously have become quite useful for educators. Some teachers find it effective to share weekly plans through email communication. In some cases, collaboration can take an even less formal approach. For example, teachers can communicate through journaling. A shared spiral, binder, or folder can be kept in a designated location in the classroom. Inside the journal, collaborating teachers can communicate regarding lesson planning goals and small group needs. In my own experience with in-class support, I found journaling to be useful in classrooms where I spent small pockets of time. This technique is also a great first

step with teachers who are hesitant about planning together.

Talk Less, Listen (and Smile) More

"There's no reason to accommodate anything. Everyone will get the same instruction."

"Ian has been here since the beginning of the year. I've heard him talking with his friends. He speaks English just fine. He doesn't need accommodations in my math class. He'll get the same instruction everyone else gets. It's not fair to give him anything different."

"If I spend time accommodating for a couple of ELs, I am taking away instructional time from all the other students."

"Accommodating is your job, not mine. I put the worksheets in your mailbox on Friday. Do you have them ready?"

These are actual statements I have heard from teachers. Some have stopped me in my tracks, eyes wide, heart pounding, mouth gaping. And my first instinct is to tell them everything they should know about English learners and how to teach ELs. But it always helps to take a deep breath and assume that we are all coming from a place of wanting to do what's best for all of our students.

You may have heard similar remarks when trying to collaborate with teachers as you try to serve ELs who need support to access grade-level curriculum. How do we work together with reluctant teachers like the ones above to ensure that students receive adequate and equitable instruction? I have found success with starting from a place of empathy, talking less, and listening more, as well as remembering to start small (Knight, 2016).

ELs should receive grade-level curricula, yes. However, this often leaves general education teachers with the misconception that merely covering the curriculum is enough. Then when students are not successful in the classroom, everyone is left feeling frustrated. Collaborative practices work to ensure that we help ELs to *uncover* the curriculum. As the National Education Association (2015) points out:

> There is nothing wrong with English Language Learners—no deficit to fix. They are whole students we must reach and teach in ways that open their minds to the amazing possibilities of their lives, and language must not be a barrier to that goal (p. 19).

Listening more when you feel passionate and fired up is hard, but it can change the course of direction for future collaborative practices with teachers. Provide the teacher with time and space to share what they have to say while listening without responding. Listen carefully without interrupting. Even if you feel like you have the perfect answer or the perfect justification, hold it back. Just listen (and smile). After listening well, ask one question. It might be something such as, "What's the real challenge here for you?" Then listen again. A follow-up question may be, "How can I help?"

In my experience, I've noticed that many teachers who do not accommodate instruction for ELs or are reluctant about collaborating to make accommodations hesitate because they feel inadequate with instructional methods for teaching ELs. Some may have had little preservice training or minimal professional learning on the topic. No matter the circumstances, I have been met with greater success when I've approached reluctant teachers with a collegial, partnering mindset rather than opposition.

In her book, *Pathways to Greatness for ELL Newcomers,* Dr. Yzquierdo (2017) describes her own experiences as a biology teacher struggling to make content comprehensible for her EL students. As a general education teacher, one strategy she used was observing ESL teachers and incorporating the instructional techniques into her biology class. In this case, the teachers trusted one another, honored each other's knowledge, put students first, and believed in the power of collaborative practices.

Aim for Parity

In some classrooms, two teachers work in the same space to serve students. This can either be through "in-class support," sometimes called "push-in," or through a "co-teaching" model. In-class support and co-teaching have similarities and differences. Typically, in-class support is defined as short periods of time daily or weekly during which a special programs teacher comes into a general education classroom to assist and accommodate instruction. In-class support can be offered by certified teachers as well as paraprofessionals or teacher's assistants. While they often have limited or no common planning, teaching, or assessing, the two educators collaborate to share students and have common goals for student success. Robert Villa et al. (2008) describe co-teaching, on the other hand, as involving "...the distribution of responsibility among people for planning, instruction, and evaluation for a classroom of students" (p. 50). Co-teaching is a more permanent marriage between educators. The special programs teacher and the mainstream teacher work in tandem to lesson plan regularly, teach side-by-side, co-create assessments, and evaluate student success together. No matter the model, it is in the best interest of all stakeholders that both teachers

understand their roles and are agreeable to the relationship. When one or both teachers do not understand the roles or disagree with the relationship, reluctance may arise.

Special programs teachers who go into classrooms to support students and teachers can be relegated to "helping hands" if careful and purposeful instruction planning is not in place. For a special programs teacher who has a degree and much knowledge in a specialized field, being relegated to the sidelines can lead to feelings of uselessness, unhappiness, loneliness, disengagement, and more. From the general education teacher's perspective, having another teacher in the classroom who is not participating in instruction, planning, or assessment can manifest feelings that include division, hierarchy, and resentment.

Factors that contribute to reluctance to allow special programs teachers to participate with parity in classroom instruction include:

- Lack of training or understanding regarding collaborative practices
- Misconceptions about collaborative teaching practices
- Feeling the need to have complete control over classroom instruction

Reaching parity in classroom spaces takes time, trust, and intentionality. The table on the next page outlines the many small but powerful ways that collaborative partners have found success with reaching parity.

Suggestions to Consider to Promote Parity	Benefits for All Stakeholders
Place both teachers' names on the door.	Tells families and students that the classroom is a shared space.
Have a desk or designated space for each teacher in the classroom.	Makes both educators feel comfortable and welcome.
Introduce both teachers as classroom teachers from the beginning of the year.	Increases the chances that students will see both educators as equals.
Send home a letter to families sharing why the class has two teachers and who they are.	Enhances parental understanding of co-teaching or in-class support.
Ensure that groups are flexible.	Reduces stigma on students.
Include both teachers in parent-teacher conferences with families of English learners.	Allows everyone to consistently get the same message.
Attend professional learning opportunities as a pair.	Builds instructional consistency.

Share the Spotlight

In some situations, special programs teachers may find that mainstream teachers feel they need to have control of instruction. The raw truth is that sometimes this happens when mainstream teachers do not feel confident in special programs teachers' capabilities in content instruction. The feeling may stem from mainstream teachers who have not seen special programs teachers teach or plan and the circumstance often leads to mainstream teachers who do not embrace collaborative practices. Understanding our roles and how they intersect can help

us work together effectively. After all, we can't teach content without language, and furthermore, teaching language is most effective and engaging when it's tied authentically to content. The two go hand-in-hand. A general education teacher strives to teach content but uses language to deliver the information (Salva & Matis, 2017).

Sharing the spotlight means that both educators provide students with the time and space to explore content and language through academic and linguistic lenses. These experiences allow all students to grapple with ideas and negotiate for

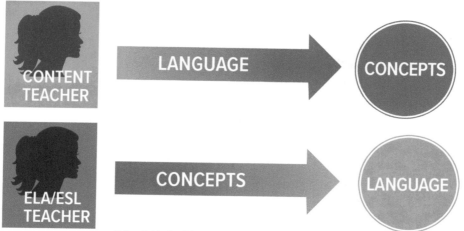

Salva & Matis, 2017, p. 58. Used with permission.

meaning in their own way. English learners are not the only students learning new language structures and vocabulary in classrooms.

The goal of ESL/ELD teachers is to develop language, but they use content as a means to achieve that goal. While both teachers use both language and content, each has a different end in mind. Working collaboratively will help ensure that students seamlessly make both linguistic and academic progress. I imagine a bicycle. Both the wheels and the handlebars are important. They each have their own job, yet they work in tandem to achieve the overarching goal. We, too, have an overarching goal for our students. We want them to progress as learners and become productive citizens of our global society. In order to achieve that goal, they must be ready linguistically and academically.

Many teachers have become accustomed to independently setting up their own classrooms, planning lessons, delivering instruction, conducting parent-teacher conferences, grading papers, evaluating students, and much more. Doing all these things with another teacher is novel and may take some time getting used to. Improving collaborative practices with teachers who may be reluctant about giving up the spotlight can be challenging, but it isn't a reason to give up. When a collaborating member seems to avoid sharing the spotlight, try one of these ideas for encouraging a more open mind:

- Give a compliment about an idea or lesson
- Publicly praise your peer for their work
- Leave a thank you note, even it's for the smallest thing
- Brag about a lesson they did

The simple act of giving a compliment or praise may change everything and set the partnership off in the right direction.

Promote Inclusion

Removing students from the general education classroom creates the idea that those are your students and these are mine, which breeds opposition between educators. If we continue to invite this type of setting, we foster the notion that teaching our students is not a joint effort, and this encourages reluctance to collaborate. However, inclusion is based on the premise that teachers will recognize and respond to all students' needs (Honigsfeld & Dove, 2019).

I hear from many special programs teachers that they covet the small group pull-out time they spend with their English learners. They enjoy this time with them because they create bonds and report that their students verbalize more in these pull-out settings. I get it. I understand. And when I first started teaching ESL, we pulled students out of the classroom for long periods of time too. I remember the relationships we built and the great times we had.

While bonding and creating rich talk opportunities are critical, we want to bring these components into general education classroom settings. English learners benefit from collaborating with native English-speaking peers. Being in the general education classroom gives ELs more opportunity to learn English and content simultaneously, which can help avoid creating unintentional gaps in their education (Wright, 2015). As collaborative teachers, it's important that we promote and advocate for inclusive settings that foster cooperative learning.

Classrooms where English learners are misunderstood are often run by educators who have experienced little or no training on instructional methods that support ELs. Reluctance to collaborate with special programs teachers about serving English learners can grow from lack of training about effective teaching for ELs. For instance, when I was a young teacher, I had a student who was receiving special education services. I did not have training on how to serve students with this particular type of need. My own feelings of inadequacy led me to lean on the special education teacher's strengths. I often deferred to sending him to work with the special education teacher rather than staying to work with his peers or getting to know him because I felt that I lacked the ability to help him.

The problem with this way of thinking is that inadequacies can manifest into what seem like students' deficits. In essence, students suffer, and the collaboration between teachers continues to be strained. Removing students from the classroom can have several detrimental effects:

- Embarrass the student who's asked to leave
- Create gaps in content learning
- Reduce social relationships
- Stigmatize students who are removed

Students who are segregated out of the classroom for instruction are sent strong nonverbal messages that they do not belong with their peers or that they are not capable of learning from the same teacher that all the other students can learn from. The toll that removing students out of the classroom can take may be long-term.

STUDENT SUCCESS STORIES

Plan for Success

As an ESL teacher who visited multiple classrooms daily to co-teach and deliver in-class support, my schedule was always changing based on students' needs. One year, I visited Mrs. Hodges' fifth-grade classroom for only 15 minutes daily. While 15 minutes may seem like a short amount of time, when we plan for success, we can maximize it.

At first, Mrs. Hodges and I had a hard time figuring out how to maximize our time together. We wanted to make sure that, even though it wasn't a lengthy chunk, we used it wisely. Mrs. Hodges ran a reader's workshop classroom, which allowed for independent reading and small group instruction. As we discussed this structure, we thought about how I might support readers during the 15 minutes that I would be coming in. Mrs. Hodges explained that students were independently reading self-selected books around the room as she gathered small groups to work on strategy lessons. Together, we decided that each day when I came in, I would hold reading conferences one-on-one with three students and take anecdotal notes in a binder that she and I kept together.

We agreed to communicate through email weekly to keep in touch regarding lesson objectives. However, our main point of contact was the binder of anecdotal notes. Each day I walked into the room as the students read independently and I grabbed the binder. In this, Mrs. Hodges and I kept checklists and informal notes about our reading conferences with students. I could see on the checklist who needed a conference and who had already had one. As I conferred with a few readers, I took anecdotal notes that Mrs. Hodges used to build targeted small group instruction.

Some days, Mrs. Hodges would email to ask me to meet with specific students and look for targeted skills, but every day, we kept communication via a journal with our anecdotal notes and charts of who I had conferred with and who needed a conference. On a weekly basis, I met with 10 to 15 students to talk about their reading, set goals, and take notes that would support targeted small group instruction. It worked beautifully. Students were being heard, and the needle was moving because we created a routine and a collaborative plan for success.

If Mrs. Hodges and I did not create this plan for success, it would have been easy for me to come in and be relegated to the sidelines. I could have milled around the room and flown by the seat of my pants just doing what I could each day. But instead, we made a conscious effort together to do what was best for our students.

Share the Spotlight

Mr. Bird was a fourth-grade math teacher who was not ESL certified. That year, our campus experienced an influx of newcomer students in fourth grade. Since our model for serving newcomer EL students included both pull-out and in-class support, I spent part of my day working with a group of fourth-grade ELs in both settings. I had never taught fourth-grade math myself, but as an in-class support teacher, I was learning the standards very quickly.

Mr. Bird and I met before the start of the school year to talk about our newfound relationship as collaborative partners. My hope was for him to know that I was there to work with him and to serve all students. I wanted to be an active member in the classroom setting, and I was eager to learn all I could about fourth-grade math!

Well, our first meeting did not go as well as I pictured in my mind. My excitement was not met with the same eagerness to collaborate. Mr. Bird was quick to let me know that there was no need to plan together (even though we had a common planning time). He explained that I could "look at" his lesson plans online but that they were always the same: topic (for example, equations), page from the book, and which problems the students would do. Here's where I had to take some deep breaths.

I left that initial meeting with my shoulders slumped and my head hanging. You are probably thinking, how is this a success story? Well, it was, but I had to choose to make it one. Through continued patience and developing understanding of Mr. Bird's personality, I began to build a relationship with him. I took any opportunity Mr. Bird would afford me, and I ran with it. I began thinking about our initial meeting. Rather than focusing on what went wrong, I thought about what went right. He allowed me access to his lesson plans. That was one step in the right direction. Now, what could I do with the lesson plans? I decided I would get to know the lessons in advance to ensure that I could pull small groups to build academic language and vocabulary. While the class worked independently on the assignment Mr. Bird had given, I worked with a small group of students inside the classroom on the same assignment. We used visuals, real objects, and sentence stems, and we held structured conversations about the work. The group was flexible and consisted of ELs and non-ELs. There were even days when some additional students would ask if they could join our small group because they wanted some extra help.

Over time, Mr. Bird began to feel comfortable with me in his room. He noticed that students were making greater progress in math using the new strategies. Eventually, he was comfortable enough to let me teach whole group lessons and let me put up a math word wall with visuals that stayed in his room.

Overall, I counted this as a success. Not only did English learners gain language and math skills that year, but English speakers also benefited, and along the way Mr. Bird and I both learned a lot from one another as well.

Promote Inclusion

Ruby arrived with her family from Mexico at the beginning of her fourth-grade school year. She qualified for bilingual services; however, her family opted to receive support through the ESL program. Ruby was performing at beginner levels of English proficiency, according to the language assessments she was administered upon entry. Spanish assessments showed that her literacy in her primary language was very high.

Ruby presented herself as a wide-eyed, eager-to-learn student. She carried a book with her most everywhere she went, and I began to notice that she held a new book each day. It was easy to see that Ruby loved reading, plus she benefited from learning from her grade-level peers.

Though Ruby initially tested at the beginning level of English proficiency, her progress in language acquisition was accelerated. It was clear that pulling her out of the classroom was not as beneficial for her anymore. She needed to hear native English speakers and academic English. During a collaborative meeting, her teachers discussed the options. Typically in this district, students like Ruby would continue to receive ELD through pull-out instruction. Her teacher was hesitant about making a change. Would Ruby be successful in the general education classroom? Could the teacher accommodate instruction enough to support Ruby's language needs? After looking through the formative assessments we'd gathered and knowing the drive we saw in Ruby herself, we both agreed to make sure that Ruby spent as much time in the classroom receiving grade-level curriculum as possible, with me in the room to support language acquisition.

During language arts, I met with Ruby through reading conferences and I asked her about her books. One day she asked me for a book recommendation. We went to the bookshelf together, and I showed her a few of my favorite books. She took one of the books I shared with her. The next day when she came to class, she smiled, holding the book and nodding. I couldn't believe she'd finished the whole book in one night! Then she asked for another book. This child ate books! I mean, she read everything she could get her hands on. We shared recommendations and enjoyed talking about what she'd read.

Ruby came in with beginner level English proficiency, yet by the end of the year she had passed all 3 of her standardized state tests. Her teacher and I attributed this growth to the inclusive environment that allowed Ruby to feel valued and motivated to learn.

●●● CONCLUSION

We can't expect that collaborative practices will be perfect experiences. We are not perfect people or perfect educators, but one thing we can do is intentionally plan to create time and space for working with our colleagues because ultimately, our goal is not about us, it's about serving our students.

References and Further Resources

Brown, B. (2018). *Dare to lead: Brave work. Tough conversations. Whole hearts.* Random House.

Calderón, M. E., Dove, M. G., Staehr Fenner, D., Gottlieb, M., Honigsfeld, A., Ward Singer, T., Slakk, S. M., Soto, I., & Zacarian, D. (2019). *Breaking down the wall: Essential shifts for English learners' success.* Corwin.

Honigsfeld, A. & Dove, M. G. (2019). *Collaborating for English learners: A foundational guide to integrated practices* (2nd ed.). Corwin.

Knight, J. (2016). *Better conversations: Coaching ourselves and each other to be more credible, caring, and connected.* Corwin.

National Education Association. (2015). *How educators can advocate for English language learners: All in!* https://www.colorincolorado.org/sites/default/files/ELL_AdvocacyGuide2015.pdf

Salva, C., & Matis, A. (2017). *Boosting achievement: Reaching students with interrupted or minimal education.* Seidlitz Education.

Staehr Fenner, D., & Snyder, S. (2017). *Unlocking English learners' potential: Strategies for making content accessible.* Corwin.

Villa, R. A., Thousand, J. S., & Nevin, A. I. (2008). *A guide to co-teaching: Practical tips for facilitating student learning* (2nd ed.). Corwin.

Wright, W. E. (2015). *Foundations for teaching English language learners: Research, theory, policy, and practice* (2nd ed.). Caslon Publishing.

Yzquierdo, M. (2017). *Pathways to greatness for ELL newcomers: A comprehensive guide for schools & teachers.* Seidlitz Education.

9

Return
to Better

POST-PANDEMIC
COLLABORATION
PRACTICES

Kristina Robertson
Andrea Honigsfeld
& Maria G. Dove

Collaborating on a joint project like this volume
required a lot of teamwork, coordination, and a shared
understanding of what we wished to accomplish. When
we realized that COVID-19 would delay the final steps
that could bring this book to our readers, we decided we
needed to tell one more story! We knew we were all living
through history that would be analyzed and discussed
for decades, if not centuries to come, and we had an
irresistible urge to reconnect with our authors and learn
how they had continued to collaborate for the sake of
their English learners/multilingual learners (ELs/MLs) during
COVID-19.

We reached out to each author to check in on how they
were doing in their respective schools, cities, states, and
countries and whether or not any form of collaboration
and instruction was continuing in support of multilingual
learners. We were deeply concerned about how the
educators featured in this book—educators everywhere,
in fact—were able to manage their daily responsibilities
of teaching and supporting their students remotely while
adjusting to the uncertainties of ever-changing guidelines
and instructional delivery modes. We were sincerely
hoping no one had to struggle through these difficult times
alone and that some sort of professional collaboration
could be sustained. With this in mind, we contacted our
authors to get their insights on lessons learned from
their collaboration and instructional delivery during
the pandemic.

We wanted to uncover the experiences our authors had with teaching remotely, how they sustained their collaboration and instruction through weeks and months of isolation, and if there was any continuity to previously established partnerships and successful practices. We also wanted to investigate whether or not any new opportunities were emerging to collaboratively support each other's work as well as students' learning. Moreover, we wondered if teacher collaboration had actually become one of the most important support systems of the pandemic.

WHAT DID WE LEARN?

We invited our authors to submit responses to a survey asking about the collaborative practices they experienced during the pandemic and the outcomes from this work. The survey prompts were as follows:

Are you collaborating now, and how are you doing it in this new environment? Please share briefly if you have any rich experiences.

What has changed, and what has remained the same when it comes to serving ELs/MLs in your context?

What has been the most challenging, yet memorable, experience you have had as an educator during the pandemic that called for collaboration, joint intervention, or any form of a collaborative solution?

The Chinese word for "crisis" is composed of two characters: one signifying "danger"

and the other, "opportunity." In what ways have you seen opportunities for collaboration somehow growing out of these most dangerous and challenging times?

We are all interconnected and responsible for each other. In times of trouble, teachers, families, and students are especially tuned in to what is fair and equitable, and there is a special call to action to be even more responsive to the unique challenges everyone faces. In your context, what purposeful collaborative efforts have been put in place that advocated for a more equitable education for all?

Our authors painted a picture of struggle and triumph. Their most frequently used words to describe their experiences were "overwhelmed," "collaborative," "focused," "connected," "advocacy," and "opportunity." Educators were making history around the world, and we all experienced massive changes to educational settings virtually overnight. We could see from our authors' responses that teachers and leaders rose to the challenge. In this chapter, we explore their insights on successful collaboration, effective strategies, and guidance for future practices. To best organize the experiences our authors shared with us, we divided this chapter into four sections:

1) **What Did Collaboration Success Look Like?**

2) **What Contributed to Success or Presented Challenges?**

3) **What Strategies and Tools Worked for Teams?**

4) **How Can Collaboration Shape the Future of Education for ELs/MLs?**

> "Since we are all experiencing this crisis together, it seems as if many who were hesitant to allow others into their space are now inviting it. I have witnessed an unbelievable synergy among teachers that I had never seen before."
> - Michelle Gill

What Did Collaboration Success Look Like?

Michelle Gill and many other authors affirmed that overall, collaboration was successful and had increased during the pandemic. Co-planning was more important, and it happened more frequently and through multiple methods, such as texting, Zoom, and phone calls. Many of our authors noted that teams who had positive collaboration experiences prior to the pandemic enhanced their collaborative practices during it. Sarah Bouwer and Tan Huynh were among them:

> We had nurtured our relationship in such a way that we trusted what each other would do and knew that each person would be intentional about building on the other person's strengths. As a result, our garden plot continued to grow and flourish even in the midst of a challenging circumstance.

Starting with a trusting collaboration relationship gave some teams a head start, although other teams that had collaborated little prior to the pandemic built trust through a sense of urgency to meet ELs/MLs' learning needs. Our authors confirmed that requests for collaboration from general education teachers increased during the pandemic because many classroom teachers were overwhelmed as they tried to meet the needs of learners through technology.

Collaboration teams working remotely developed diverse ways of communicating and planning instruction to benefit ELs/MLs. Authors described strategies for collaboration success that emphasized honoring co-planning as sacred time, maintaining flexibility in when and how to connect, using a variety of digital tools for communication and instruction, and drawing on each others' strengths for effective instruction. We will explore each of these strategies in-depth.

Multiple authors mentioned prioritizing co-planning as essential and described the numerous ways teachers were very intentional in using planning time. Jane Russell Valezy noted this trend in her responses:

> Some teachers who may not usually reach out and generally prefer to work independently have begun to approach us for support in this "crisis mode," which has

opened up doors for further collaboration. We set a regular day/time to meet and kept it. [We] looked at our combined responsibilities and made sure we scheduled enough co-planning time each week to effectively complete lessons and tasks.

Teams often had one day and time of the week set aside for planning, or the school's schedule was set up to give the team a common preparation time. Part of maximizing this sacred planning time was focusing on instructional goals and learning objectives. Jackie Griffin and Stephanie Just described the strong sense of purpose around collaborative instruction, saying, "We find the most success for our students when all staff who are serving that student come together to analyze the data and collaborate on next steps." Michelle Gill supported this statement as well:

Teachers who established a co-planning schedule had success instructing together because they were on the same page about their roles and the lesson outcomes. Many co-planning teams met weekly or developed a more fluid check-in/planning system throughout the week using digital tools.

Jackie and Stephanie described how digital tools added flexibility to teachers' ability to communicate and plan instruction. "Luckily," they said, "Zoom makes it very easy for us to connect with one another quickly for next steps that make each student's education equitable." Co-planning became more flexible due to electronic tools such as Zoom, text messaging, and Google Docs. In addition, the digital tools allowed teachers to connect much more fluidly, making it easier to check in quickly at regular intervals. While these digital tools were implemented to support remote student learning, they provided multiple new ways for teaching teams to stay connected as well.

One of the most heartening themes was the authors' description of how remote collaboration allowed them to expand their network, learn from each other, and take more risks instructionally as they tried new strategies. Jackie and Stephanie explained it well:

Prior to this challenging time, educators in our district wished they had more time to observe and learn from each other. Zoom has given us the gift of joining another classroom with just the click of a button. We are able to collaborate with people in our building as well as educators across the district, both those with similar jobs and those from other grades and roles.

The opportunity to learn about colleagues' strengths and draw on them instructionally was very powerful. Michelle shared that, "Collaborative partnerships grew stronger as teacher teams navigated difficult challenges in the pandemic and gained a deeper understanding of the strengths each teacher brought to the partnership." Even though the pandemic added stress to teachers' plates, our authors saw this as a growth opportunity. Tan affirmed this notion: "I was actually quite excited regarding virtual school as it allowed us to lean into each other's strengths, and I knew it was a great opportunity to grow." There was an underlying understanding that teachers could work smarter, not harder, by relying on the strengths of others and using planning and instructional time strategically. Allyson, John, and Ashley emphasized this idea as well: "Strengths-based collaboration not only values both parties' skills and experience, but it's also more efficient and effective." One outcome of this positive attitude was a strong definition of specific instructional roles and responsibilities. For example, when planning, Allyson, John, and Ashley asked themselves, "How are we both truly present in remote instruction, whether synchronous or asynchronous?" Teachers made collaborative practices work because they understood the value of connecting with others' expertise and incorporating co-instruction to ensure that all students received support.

While the pandemic forced educators into crisis implementation of virtual instruction, those who embraced collaborative planning were able to provide quality instruction for ELs/MLs. A silver lining of remote learning was that authors reported much more focus on academics than behavior. Educators were able to truly experience the benefits of academic co-planning without being sidetracked by pressing behavior concerns. It is clear that collaborative planning done well — focused on academics and with committed, growth-minded educators — greatly benefitted both teachers and students during pandemic learning.

Educators were able to truly experience the benefits of academic co-planning without being sidetracked by pressing behavior concerns.

● ● ●

"When you have two people who have a strong relationship grounded in trust and respect and who have actively nurtured that relationship, I think the sky's the limit for collaborative opportunities."
- Sarah Bouwer and Tan Huynh

What Contributed to Success or Presented Challenges?

Many things contributed to successful collaboration in the pandemic. In addition to the elements listed earlier, collaborative teams were successful when there was a high level of trust, an attitude of gratitude, agreement about the collaborative partnership, and a shared responsibility for family communication and advocacy. Sarah and Tan described increased risk-taking as a benefit of collaborative instruction in a totally new environment. Sarah explained, "Because we had a strong relationship grounded in vulnerability and trust, I knew I could take risks and try things, and there would be no judgment if it flopped." The fact that few had ever taught under these conditions using online tools empowered collaborators to work creatively and allowed them to learn together. "Realizing that we simply can't do it all individually is tough," Katie explained, "but we are so fortunate to have forged strong partnerships so we can rely on each other for both personal and professional support."

Effective collaborators ensured that each person understood their roles and responsibilities, and these undertakings became even more important once remote instruction started. If teachers could not physically be in a room together to do quick verbal or nonverbal check-ins about how a lesson or activity was going, they needed to develop a strong script for online co-instruction because they didn't have the normal in-person cues. Allyson, John, and Ashley expressed this change in instructional delivery in their comment, "Additionally, when we can only collaborate remotely, it's imperative that co-teachers are able to rely on each other to accomplish their agreed-upon responsibilities." They went on to underscore the important connection between co-planning and co-teaching: "We always say there is no co-teaching without co-planning, and that is even more true remotely."

Collaborative teams also used digital tools to maximize intentional connections with multilingual families. Allyson, John, and Ashley shared their enthusiastic embrace of this new opportunity:

> We are not prone to implementing half-measures, so we blew the door off of any limitations our previous parent communication norms held. Whenever information needs to be sent out, we utilize multiple communication avenues, such as our digital classrooms, ClassDojo, and TalkingPoints, and we ensure that all home languages are represented.

Multilingual parents were at a disadvantage in the remote learning environment due to the technology gap many experienced as well as to a lack of understanding of the content and how their children needed to learn in this new structure. And yet, family members became more integral to their child's learning success, and they needed to be able to connect with teachers regarding both learning expectations and their child's progress. Allyson, John, and Ashley added more "family office hours" to support parents with their children's remote learning at home. They explained, "Opening up your office hours to families allows for them to be involved in the students' education and helps them when they are teaching at home." Communicating and developing relationships with multilingual families was a shared responsibility between EL and general education teachers. This mutual engagement with students' families led to a deeper understanding of the need for all educators to be advocates for EL/ML students and families. Michelle shared this priority in her district: "...we have focused on ensuring all educators embrace and understand their role as advocates." Some schools had structures in place that enhanced teachers' abilities to build relationships and communicate with families. Jackie and Stephanie described how "looping" their grade level from one grade to the next with the same teachers "allowed us, as a collaborative team, to consistently communicate with our families and plan out in advance how we intended to stay connected in a virtual space."

Our authors also reported that they became greater advocates when they saw student and family challenges firsthand while engaging in distance learning. Teachers who may have had minimal experience with an EL/ML student's daily life now understood in intimate ways how many barriers some faced. Jane described how her observation of students' home and academic needs increased her desire to support them. "Another part of my responsibilities that increased in importance during virtual learning was advocating on behalf of students."

Not everything related to collaboration generated positive results, however. Our authors identified several challenges that arose during the pandemic. In some cases, co-planning and co-teaching took a backseat during remote learning because many teachers felt overwhelmed. This inability to collaborate left EL teachers feeling disconnected and even more responsible for the success of ELs/MLs. Valentina described the frustration EL teachers felt when left out of collaborative teacher meetings because general education teachers were overwhelmed. As a result, students weren't receiving accommodations to support their learning. In addition, Valentina discussed how the EL teachers had the responsibility to supply English language support and strategies whenever possible, but without a collaborative space and with the intense stress teachers were feeling, they were shut out of the planning process.

There were multiple complex factors that adversely impacted student learning during the pandemic, and the situation could change multiple times in a short period of time. Our authors described educational teams that didn't have the language background needed to make content lessons accessible to ELs/MLs. Moreover, supporting newcomer students was extremely challenging given their limited English language and technology skills. Teachers had to work exceptionally hard to mitigate all the factors that limited students' learning, yet even their best efforts sometimes weren't enough to overcome the lack of student engagement, as Jackie and Stephanie explained:

> We've realized just how important it is to understand external factors that affect student performance. We have always known this is important to consider, but these are new situations that have never happened before...[I]t prompts us to gain an understanding of what is impacting the students' learning.

Finally, teachers who taught in-person and online simultaneously were doing double the work and needed to plan content and language instruction for both formats. This "dual-focus" instructional method was not based on research but rather born out of a crisis and desperation to reach as many students as possible while keeping people safe during the pandemic. If expectations of teachers prior to the pandemic could be described as riding a unicycle while spinning plates, then during the pandemic, it was like they were also blindfolded, juggling with one hand, and spinning plates with the other. There was a tremendous shift in instructional responsibilities; teachers needed to incorporate additional digital tools, communicate a new set of expectations to students, and devise and execute a multi-formatted approach to teaching in a profession that was already extremely demanding and formidable. These challenges are why it is even more amazing that many of our authors expressed so much positivity about collaboration—how it actually reduced the workload and increased student learning. Perhaps the very act of collaborating and the trust built during the collaboration process is a way of removing the blindfold and sharing the juggling and plate spinning responsibilities successfully.

What Strategies and Tools Worked For Teams?

All of our authors have rich experiences with collaborative planning and instructional design. In response to our pandemic survey, they shared insights on specific strategies and tools that contributed to collaboration success. A common element in all of the collaborative success stories was a commitment to collaboration and developing positive relationships that could support whatever new challenge came to the learning environment. Robert Fulghum (2003) underscored this belief in his book, *All I Needed to Know I Learned in Kindergarten,* with this simple yet powerful message: "When you go out into the world, watch out for traffic, hold hands, and stick together" (p. 14). The following list shows how teachers held hands and stuck together during the pandemic.

"To set our partnership up for success, we completed a new co-teaching contract. In many ways, virtual co-teaching is a new kind of relationship. Having tough conversations to work out the nuts and bolts was essential to starting out on the right foot."

- Allyson Caudill, John Cox, and Ashley Blackely

1. Committing to Collaboration as a Key Focus in Your Context

During the pandemic, collaborative partners continued to renew their dedication to joint planning and instruction in a variety of ways. As the pandemic unfolded, teachers needed to be flexible and respond to emerging needs very quickly. One strategy teachers relied on was setting a sacred time to meet and plan weekly (or doing so during preparation time.) Collaborative partners met at least once a week and sometimes more. During the meeting time, teachers would discuss and agree on their roles and responsibilities in the lesson, and just by maintaining this sacred time, they sent a nonverbal message that they were all in to collaborate for ELs/MLs.

2. Committing to Finding and Learning Digital Tools to Increase Effective Communication and Respond Quickly and Flexibly

Teachers desperately needed strategies to keep students and families informed of the quickly changing learning environment and expectations, so they dedicated time to teaching students and families how to access information and learn electronically. The most common tools our authors mentioned were video conferencing apps like Zoom and Google Meet; digital learning tools such as Google Workplace (formerly G Suite), Canva, Jamboard, Padlet, and Nearpod; and communication tools such as ClassDojo, Google Voice (phone), Facebook, TalkingPoints, and

district translations. This shift to using multiple digital tools was an immense amount of work for teachers, as they had to first learn and then adopt these technologies with tight turnaround times. However, it was a tremendous benefit that there were so many free, effective digital tools to maintain learning and communication. It will be very advantageous for teachers to continue using these tools and developing their skill sets in incorporating them for in-person learning.

3. Discussing Roles and Responsibilities and Maintaining Clear Expectations

Once teachers committed to collaborative planning and instruction, they needed to determine how they would work together. Many teachers can recall a time when collaboration didn't go well, and there were several reasons that was the case. Either one or more people were not committed to meeting regularly, the process was undermined by not following the agenda during meetings, team members didn't know or take seriously their roles or responsibilities, deadlines for creating or gathering resources and materials were not met, or someone took over, which resulted in a lack of teamwork. Some issues are complex and not easily solved, but others are often handled by maintaining a collaborative team agreement that clearly outlines a list of expectations for each team member. The list should be very comprehensive and include everything from, "What time do we meet?" to "How will we handle our differences?"

Allyson, John, and Ashley shared how they adapted their co-teaching preferences to suit a remote environment and developed a best practices plan to guide their decision-making:

> We always say there is no co-teaching without co-planning, and that is even more true when teaching remotely. The good news is planning can be done just as effectively from a distance. We worked together to develop schedules that allowed for live co-teaching whenever possible. When planning asynchronous learning, we recorded the lessons together. At the very minimum, we co-planned every lesson together to integrate content and language and scaffold learning tasks.

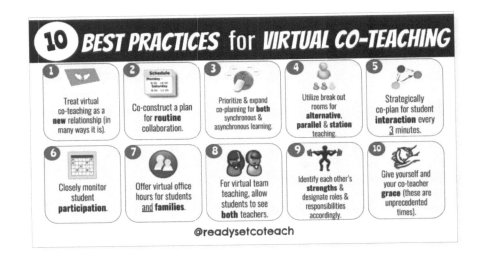

10 BEST PRACTICES for VIRTUAL CO-TEACHING

1. Treat virtual co-teaching as a **new** relationship (in many ways it is).

2. Co-construct a plan for **routine** collaboration.

3. Prioritize & expand co-planning for **both** synchronous & asynchronous learning.

4. Utilize break out rooms for **alternative, parallel & station** teaching.

5. Strategically co-plan for student **interaction** every 3 minutes.

6. Closely monitor student **participation**.

7. Offer virtual office hours for students **and families**.

8. For virtual team teaching, allow students to see **both** teachers.

9. Identify each other's **strengths** & designate roles & responsibilities accordingly.

10. Give yourself and your co-teacher **grace** (these are unprecedented times).

@readysetcoteach

4. Discussing Your Practice and Purposefully Selecting Protocols for Meeting

Michelle shared a co-planning template that guided collaborative teams to focus on academic targets and supports for ELs/MLs. As collaborative team members walked through the template, they also discussed their roles and responsibilities for planning certain activities.

As team members developed collective efficacy, they were able to plan differentiation more easily and increase creative instructional practices, as Jackie and Stephanie demonstrated: "During these unique times, we know now more than ever that students need a variety of ways to show they are engaged with both the teacher and peers." The authors described how they used digital tools, such as Nearpod and Book Creator, to offer scaffolded assignments. Selecting these

Digital
Co-Planning
Template

online tools to differentiate student work was especially helpful in serving newcomers who were overwhelmed with technology and content learning expectations. Teachers also saw evidence of students learning in new and exciting ways by using these digital tools. Michelle shared her enthusiasm about her students' language use: "To our surprise, when we incorporated student choice and the right tools, such as Nearpod and Book Creator, our language learners were speaking more than ever!"

Part of the intentional collaboration process required an agreement on why, how, and when teachers should meet. Some of our authors described how they met weekly at the same time and place, while others used Zoom or another video conferencing application to meet from home or create the flexibility to meet in the evenings. However, the collaborative partners who knew each other very well were able to simply use digital tools such as Google Docs for planning, with short text exchanges multiple times during the week to clarify and revise. One significant action was to agree on when and how teams would communicate with each other. Many described setting up Zoom meetings, while others preferred to have brief phone calls and text messages. The agreed-upon communication style needed to fit for all members of the collaborative team. Once the how had been decided, it was even more important to establish ground rules for why communication was necessary. For example, if the partners agreed that each could make changes to their own lesson activities, they could also decide that no communication was needed to address changes. However, the partners might agree that when students were struggling with learning, the teachers needed a Zoom meeting to review student work and problem-solve together.

On a final note, our authors shared the importance of determining when it was acceptable for team members to contact each other. Some teachers are morning people, and some are night owls, so in order to collaborate successfully, they expressed the need to set boundaries that would work for everyone. For example, identifying parameters such as no phone calls before 9:00 a.m. on weekends or after 8:00 p.m. on weeknights was a key factor. Everyone can relate to the "ghosted" feeling when they've sent a couple of texts and haven't received a response to their burning question. On the other hand, we also know the feeling of getting multiple texts or long voicemails that continuously interrupt us and make it difficult to focus on our work— or our personal lives. Therefore, establishing the logistics of communication ensured a healthy, happy collaborative experience.

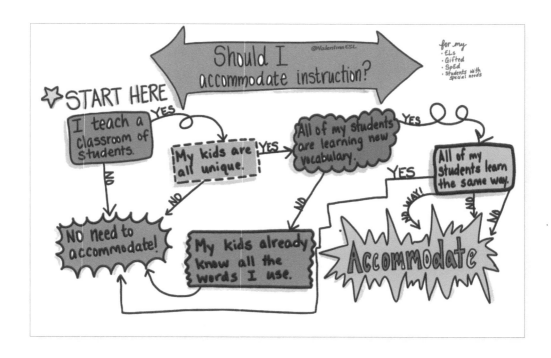

5. Planning for High Student Engagement with Both Teachers as Instructors

Collaborative teams established guidelines to increase student interaction in the online learning environment even when many students had their cameras and microphones off during remote learning. Teachers often felt as if they were talking into an empty box with pictures inside. To ensure student engagement, Allyson, John, and Ashley established the following guidelines:

> When planning lessons, we use the three-to-one rule. For every three minutes of instruction, [there is] at least one minute of interaction. Expecting students to talk, type, or tap (click) every three minutes has not only kept them engaged, but it has also made the content more accessible for students because we are chunking the material into easily digestible pieces.

Teachers often think student engagement requires labor-intensive planned activities such as academic quiz games or verbal discussion. However, the online instructional environment was very intimidating for some students, and they often preferred to stay muted. By using the mini-check system of asking students to tap or add comments in a chat box, teachers fostered student interaction and were better able to gather feedback on learning. With online instruction, it was impossible to know what was happening behind muted thumbnail photos, so teachers needed to develop new, creative ways of "knowing" the learning environment and student needs.

Students need to see their co-teachers as instructional leaders for content and language. Teachers who team teach can ensure that they regularly plan for both teachers to take the lead on presenting to the whole group of students. Yet, more differentiation can happen through small group work. Allyson, John, and Ashley recommended establishing separate spaces for individualized learning in the online classroom: "Utilize breakout rooms for alternative, parallel, and station teaching." Alternative, parallel, and station teaching are common terms in a co-teaching setting, and they can be easily implemented in online learning environments using Zoom breakout rooms. These class configurations are excellent uses of both teachers' skill sets and abilities to differentiate instruction to meet student learning needs. In the alternative approach, teachers took turns as the main presenter. In the parallel approach, they each moved to a breakout room with a select group of students and presented the same content in ways that made learning more accessible for their own group. It's worth noting that parallel teaching may be more advantageous with online learning since teachers are not distracted by the sound coming from the other side of the classroom. Lastly, station teaching allowed all students to cycle through breakout rooms to receive different instruction to support their learning. For example, one group may have focused on reading a short text, while another worked on writing a short story on the same theme. Breakout rooms can provide numerous opportunities for differentiated instruction as long as they are well thought out and implemented purposefully. Allyson, John, and Ashley described this concept perfectly:

> We now utilize breakout rooms during kids-time so that student leaders can assist their peers, students can connect over a video game, and multiple conversations can occur at the same time. Working collaboratively to design the expectations and manage the virtual spaces has allowed us to maintain a strong classroom culture during the pandemic.

6. Giving and Receiving Feedback

Collaborative instruction is a process, and it's important to keep tuning up practices to increase effectiveness and respond to changing dynamics. Providing timely, meaningful feedback to students on their work allows them to grow their knowledge while the information is still fresh in their minds, and the same is true for teachers. As part of a collaborative planning protocol, many teams established norms that they reviewed at the beginning and end of each meeting. One example was a checklist of items used to gauge the adherence to agreed-upon norms using simple ratings, such as numbers one through five or thumbs up, down, or sideways. If there was a recurring pattern, such as several low ratings for "Stay focused on the agenda and use time effectively," then the team needed to set aside time for some housekeeping and address why they were having difficulty adhering to that norm. Teams demonstrated

collective efficacy by honestly addressing issues about how they worked together and how they would continue to enjoy collaborative teaming.

Students also need specific feedback to help them understand what they need to work on to improve. Feedback is important both for in-person and online instruction, and it can be one of the trickiest things to fit into instructional time. An online learning space offers the opportunity for quick breakout sessions with individual students. In this way, no one will hear the feedback provided except the student who receives it, allowing for a private conversation to identify any misunderstandings or further support needs.

Collaborative teams often used a protocol to review student work in order to both inform instruction and provide specific, meaningful feedback to students. Allyson, John, and Ashley described the process they used, saying, "We set up a feedback-oriented learning system together to ensure we deliver feedback that is purposeful, timely, specific, and comprehensible. We implement student-friendly rubrics, checklists, and self-assessments to engage students in self-reflection." The rubrics and checklists were simple and easy to follow, so EL/ML students could conduct self or peer evaluation and offer teacher feedback as well. They did not need to restate the benchmarks from a standard; rather, they were written in kid-friendly language so students could easily examine their own work and identify where they needed more support.

7. Connecting Frequently and Developing Positive Partnerships with ML Families (Using a Language and Method that Works for Them)

Our contributing authors described how family engagement and communication with multilingual families were seen as the responsibility of both teachers using multiple methods and different languages. All teachers became proficient with multilingual communication apps such as TalkingPoints, SeeSaw, and recorded mass phone messages that had been translated into multiple languages. Through this frequent connection, teachers developed closer bonds with families and understood how strongly they desired to help their children. Allyson, John, and Ashley also explained further how they set up virtual office hours to serve families:

> Inviting families into office hours actually saved us time, and students were producing higher quality work since their parents/guardians understood the objectives and instructions. Plus, it's just another way to strengthen relationships with students' families and truly partner with them for student success.

Everyone knows that in-home, remote learning requires a lot of support from family members. For multilingual families, it often seemed like an impossible task. It was common for older children in the family to become the default tutors for their younger siblings, though this often conflicted with the older students' ability to attend to their own school work. Teaching teams that offered support to parents had a positive impact on the whole family.

8. Incorporating Social-Emotional Learning Activities into the Process

Missing from online learning was the opportunity for students to socialize with their peers through mini-connections in classes, school hallways or at recess and lunch. Students who attended class online often went from one Zoom room to another with barely a bathroom break in between. During virtual lessons, there might be breakout room time, but the online setting was intimidating for some, and it was not conducive to casual sharing and connecting. Successful teacher teams set aside student down-time with social-emotional activities, such as breathing exercises, Moodmeter check-ins, and calming videos. They also recognized the need to celebrate learning success. In one online second-grade class celebration, the students all did silly cheers as individuals shared their work and added questions to the chat box. The teacher made use of Zoom filters to have students add features such as kitty ears or a bunny nose on their screen photos.

As teachers established social-emotional activities, they explained that they were so important during virtual learning because they were perfect opportunities to discuss stress and how to handle it positively through self-care. Allyson, John, and Ashley summed this up, saying, "Give yourself, your students, and your co-teacher grace. These are challenging times."

> "There has been this realization that every student can demonstrate their learning in different ways... in their own way."
> — Michelle Gill

How Can Collaboration Shape the Future of Education for ELs/MLs?

Teachers' purposeful collaboration had a positive impact on student learning during the pandemic, and we have no doubt that continued purposeful collaboration will maintain this trend as students return to learning in physical classrooms. The challenge for educators will be to maintain a sense of urgency around academic collaboration when the crisis and anxiety have lessened. Once teachers can easily access students and monitor their learning in person, schedules will be packed, time will be short, and it will be easy to rely more on oneself than on teammates. However, pandemic or not, teammates' strengths can improve learning and impact the effectiveness of peers. Educators should beware the comfort that comes with the shift to in-person "compliance learning," meaning the "normal," pre-pandemic learning environment where ELs/MLs are perceived to be learning because they attend school. Brittany described how the pandemic situation actually improved the content of teacher team discussions,

saying, "Usually as a whole grade-level team, the challenges we discuss are more behavioral. This situation has somewhat tipped those discussions more towards academics, which is absolutely an opportunity we needed."

While many educators were frustrated by some students' frequent absences and lack of participation online, it was also a wake-up call regarding the need for individualized connections and relationship building. For some students, absences or lack of attention to learning were related to personal concerns that prevented them from being effective in online learning. But for many others, it was an opportunity to vote with their feet (or their attention) if they didn't understand the work or if it wasn't engaging or differentiated enough to allow them to be successful.

Teachers worked extremely hard to modify instruction in these challenging circumstances, and they did the best they could with minimal time and resources. Now we are climbing out of the pandemic, and it's time to "return to better." Michelle sums it up, saying, "We had to accept that there were practices in our system that were (unintentionally) marginalizing students. This was not negotiable."

In the future, educators who focus on teamwork to develop individualized academic instruction, strong relationships with ELs/MLs and their families, knowledge of students' social-emotional capacities, and culturally relevant learning environments will continue to see their students engage in learning and develop academically.

In the semesters following the pandemic, a lot of attention will be paid to learning loss and helping students "catch up," and teachers will feel immense pressure to increase student learning in a short amount of time. It seems we are always chasing some mandated target or trying to catch up to an arbitrary goal set by those in power. Teachers have the potential to reframe this narrative to talk about how students experienced interrupted learning. While they may have lost some academic learning opportunities, they also gained so much self-efficacy in new and different ways. They can navigate technology, adapt to new instructional expectations, and collaboratively problem-solve. They are stronger in their native languages and cultures thanks to their home experiences responding to the pandemic stresses. In other words, they have developed strengths they can build on when returning to the in-person classroom. Allyson, John, and Ashley shared strengths-based guiding questions for planning:

- What are our respective strengths?
- How can we use them to our advantage as we co-plan and co-instruct?
- What roles are the "best fit" for each of us?

Teachers can ask similar questions regarding their students' strengths.

The pandemic provided educators an opportunity to view students' newly developed skills as assets in classroom learning. What might this look like in a classroom post-pandemic? What if teachers reminded students of their strengths and how they problem-solved during the pandemic? What if teachers had students identify the ways they grew and became more confident as learners and then discussed with students how to use that growth in an in-person classroom setting? At the very minimum, teachers should include student assets in planning and make this known to students by referring to them during times of struggle. The phrase, "We can do hard things," comes to mind. Having prompts ready to help students get in touch with their inner strength by remembering how they were successful previously is a tremendous social-emotional and learning strategy.

The number one strategy that impacts all others is the commitment to partnering and problem-solving together. As schools "return to better," we may feel like we're paddling upstream on the Mississippi as we try to continue our collaboration work. We've created a checklist (see p. 186-187) to help collaborators continue to hone the innovative skills they developed during the pandemic. View it as a navigation tool while you paddle upstream and get to that lovely sandbar where you can rest because everything has fallen into place. Use the checklist with your team to discuss and select your areas of strength and growth to commit to moving forward. Teams are highly likely to attain goals that they've agreed to and continued to discuss progress toward achieving. The following five focus areas are followed by a corresponding checklist of strategies and tools to enhance purposeful teamwork for EL/ML success.

1. Establishing Collaborative Teaching Protocols and Trusting, Supportive Relationships

Teachers work best when they know exactly what needs to be done and they can work with a positive, supportive partner. Well, actually, we think all humans work best that way. Enough said.

2. Setting Goals and Engaging in Data Analysis to Inform Instruction

The saying goes, "What gets measured gets taught," and there's an element of truth to this. In a collaborative team, it's important that both teachers understand the instructional goal and performance expectations as well as how they will use the student work (data) collected to revise instructional practices or reteach concepts.

3. Creatively Using Digital Tools to Increase Student Engagement and Individualized Instruction

As students return to in-person instruction and regularly attend school, continue using digital tools they became comfortable with during the pandemic. Students will need these technology skills if there is another switch to remote learning, and there are likely to be students quarantined at various times during the school year until COVID-19 is (mostly) eradicated. Continuing to explore digital tools together in the classroom allows teachers to support EL/ML students in person as they engage in digital learning.

4. Developing Strong Partnerships with ML Families

One of the most obvious gaps at the beginning of the pandemic (and there were many to choose from) was the lack of effective, systemic communication with multilingual families. Federal law requires school districts to communicate in a language and method parents fully understand, and yet so many parents were in the dark about their children's learning programs—and had been for quite a while. This problem highlights how much inequity exists when communication is not conducted in a language the parents understand. What's more, educators are missing out on opportunities to offer valuable home support if they cannot connect meaningfully with parents. For this reason, it is imperative that teachers leverage communication tools and creative outreach methods to further develop partnerships with multilingual families. Katie shared her district's practices for developing partnerships with families:

> My school district has been very intentional about partnering and connecting with families and the broader community to ensure that they have opportunities to share input, needs, and challenges. Our Director of Equity and Inclusion has hosted and initiated many community meetings to both share and gather information from family/community participants.

Family engagement activities designed to involve and inform parents correlate with student success. Family engagement can be a win-win for all.

5. Attending to Self-Care and the Social-Emotional Learning of Students

They might be somewhat overstated, but the safety directions on airplanes really are applicable everywhere: "Put your own oxygen mask on before you attend to others." Teaching is a stressful job without a pandemic, or recovery from a pandemic, or whatever other crises teachers need to mitigate. Self-care has come to the surface as a major need in the caring professions during this disaster. The need was always there; educators just felt more compelled to "lean in" and ignore it until now. Yet, your classroom is a child's learning space, and your mood impacts the vibe in that space. Although it's impossible to be "on" all the time, your chances to positively affect the atmosphere in your class will be greater if you get enough sleep, eat well,

and socialize with friends and family to enhance your own well-being. Having a plan for self-care is not an overnight process—your life is a work in progress, and it's always going to be a struggle to balance your professional responsibilities and your care for your students with your own self-care. However, self-care does not need to be a spa weekend; in fact, it is most effective when sprinkled throughout each day. Therefore, consider the following:

- Take a mini walk around the building for a different perspective
- Go outdoors for some fresh air
- Do breathing exercises to maintain or enhance your calm
- Stay hydrated
- Close the door and rest in the dark quiet of your room for 10 minutes
- Eat lunch without multitasking

Attending to self-care is important for you and your students. You can also model self-care and enhance your students' social-emotional learning by promoting the need for physical, mental, and emotional health, discussing how to respond to strong emotions positively, and introducing breathing techniques or yoga. One fourth-grade teacher always had her students come in from recess and put their heads down on their desks. She walked through the classroom reading to them and stopping occasionally to lift a student's arm and shake it lightly. She said her students were ready to begin when she found enough "noodle arms." Be creative, have fun, and stay well.

COLLABORATIVE PRACTICES COMMITMENT CHECKLIST

The following checklist can be used to identify a team's and individual member's strengths and challenges and lead to setting goals. Designate a person on the team who is the most organized and efficient to keep the group focused on agreed-upon tasks. Ask another member to model new strategies or begin the meeting with a warm-up. Having roles and responsibilities to guide teamwork and group learning is a large part of the collaborative process. Using the following checklist will guide and support your conversations and strengthen team efforts.

1) Establish Collaborative Teaching Protocols and Trusting, Supportive Relationships

☐ Consider collaboration meetings as sacred time

☐ Establish roles and responsibilities for each member of the team

☐ Strive for equitable and balanced co-teaching partnerships

☐ Develop problem-solving protocols/processes

☐ Create joyful learning experiences

☐ Be vulnerable—have each others' backs and become a trustworthy partner

☐ Invest in the relationship

2) Set Goals and Engage in Data Analysis to Inform Instruction

☐ Determine the learning target as a team

☐ Collect student work and assessment data to demonstrate learning

☐ Analyze data to inform instruction and determine whether to move forward, add supports, or reteach

☐ Discuss instructional practices and roles to determine teacher strengths and areas of growth to support EL/ML instruction

3) Creatively Use Digital Tools to Increase Student Engagement and Individualized Instruction

☐ Implement community-building time by creating breakout groups for informal student-to-student chats

☐ Discover what tools students like to use, and include them in instruction – tools like Google Jamboard, Padlets, Zoom annotation, polls, and games enliven the learning space and create connections between students while demonstrating learning

4) Develop Strong Partnerships with ML Families

☐ Use a variety of methods to connect frequently (at least once a month) with each ML family to share insights on their child's learning and strengths— digital tools such as a Google Voice phone number, TalkingPoints, or Zoom allow you to text or talk in multiple languages

☐ Discover how your ML families best receive information: phone, text, visit, hard copy, or electronic school newsletter

☐ Translate written information for families who are literate in their home languages. Reach families with underdeveloped literacy in their home languages by phone or social media with audio or visuals

5) Attend to Self-Care and the Social-Emotional Learning of Students

☐ Remember that a child's learning environment is created by the teacher

☐ Take care of your own physical, mental, and emotional health and reduce stress levels in order to create a positive, effective learning space for all students

☐ Incorporate social-emotional learning opportunities for students to connect with peers around meaningful topics and give them opportunities to share concerns and questions

☐ Create classroom rituals that affirm and reduce students' stress levels

Develop Strong Partnerships with ML Families (As told by Kristina)

It is easy to focus on the educational crises brought on by pandemic learning, such as the lack of technology and access to WiFi, teachers' lack of training in online instruction and digital tools, constantly shifting educational settings, and so on. However, it is important to recognize the strengths that emerged as well. Sian, an eighth-grader, is an example of a student who was underestimated by everyone—even those who knew him well and believed in him. He is a Bhutanese refugee, dual-identified as EL and a student with disabilities, In person, his daily schedule included two special education classes, an EL class, and a paraprofessional to attend his other classes with him. As our district moved quickly to online learning in grades K through 12, his teachers worried about how he would be able to learn in such a complex virtual environment. His mother has limited English and technology skills but is a fierce advocate for her son, and together they were determined to be successful. Many hours of Zoom meetings and phone calls occurred at the beginning of the online learning program. Sian had many questions and experienced frustration trying to remember all the different areas to visit for various classes and assignments. However, he quickly began to advocate for himself. He used teacher office hours to call directly and get help navigating a class webpage or discuss assignments he was having difficulty with. Soon, his teachers were amazed to see that Sian was not only navigating his own digital work well, but he was also providing guidance and leadership to other students who were having difficulty. Sometimes, a teacher would put Sian and another student in a breakout room so he could help problem-solve and support the student who was struggling with technology. Since he was learning at home, his mother was right by his side for every lesson. He had lost his paraprofessional support once instruction moved online, but the teachers were able to help Sian's mother advocate to become both his personal aide through the county and his official home care aide. She took her roles very seriously, and as she learned things about technology or upcoming events at the school, she informed other parents in the Bhutanese community. I spoke with Sian this spring about his online learning experience, and he said he really liked it. "In online learning, I can take time to view videos many times so I can understand, and I can always talk to my teachers because they have office hours. I feel more comfortable at home, and I feel really good about my learning this year." Sian graduated from eighth grade and is headed for ninth grade. He has demonstrated many strengths that will serve him well as he transitions to the "big time" high school. He is a persistent, creative problem-solver, he has excellent family support and a loving community, and he knows that connecting with teachers about assignments will enhance his learning. We never want to dump kids into a chaotic situation and tell them to just figure things out, but it is a beautiful thing to watch when we fear students are in over their heads and they blow past our expectations. It would certainly make for a good class discussion to talk about all the ways that students were able to grow and gain strength during the pandemic.

CO-TEACHING SUCCESS STORY

Plan for Success (As told by Kristina)

We have had co-teaching teams at the secondary level in my district for eight years. Prior to the pandemic, these teams had difficulty finding time to meet for planning and usually had just one full day each trimester to sketch out units and objectives for *the whole trimester*. The pandemic changed that dynamic, and with an asynchronous learning day, a high school co-teaching team saw an opportunity for regular, timely co-planning time. The teachers (Lara, an EL teacher, and Sharon, a social studies teacher) planned to meet every Friday for an hour and implemented the success strategies mentioned earlier in this chapter. They honored the co-planning process and held that time sacred, they set learning goals based on student work analysis, and they made space in the online classroom for breakout rooms and informal chats with each teacher. They frequently communicated by text for updates on lesson ideas, personal experiences like family events, and things that stressed them out. As they worked together regularly and formed their vision for the course, they discovered new strengths in each other and new ways to connect with parents. Lara, the EL teacher, showed Sharon how to use the district interpreter app so she could easily contact parents in multiple languages from her phone (without her personal number showing up) whenever it was convenient for her. Together, they formed a stronger partnership with parents and established a plan for connecting with them about their child's progress. The asynchronous instruction planning day was just as busy as the regular instructional days, except it involved back-to-back meetings, but both teachers felt it was such a relief to have time to plan. Once the school district returned to in-person instruction with a hybrid model that included a Friday "home learning day," they both committed to continuing with planning time because they saw how much it benefitted their work and the student learning experience.

●●● CONCLUSION

Storytelling is an ancient tradition of not only entertaining those around us but capturing and passing along vital information, lessons learned, and shared values. It also provides opportunities to celebrate successes in life. Stories from the classroom are particularly powerful since they invite readers to vicariously experience educators' instructional practices and student successes through descriptions of big ideas and subtle details, memorable teachable moments, and student voices—all of which may lead to readers reflecting on their own practices! Our goal with this volume has been to share powerful narratives about collaborative practices to support MLs and invite our readers to consider their own forms of collaboration in order to develop learning situations that engage all students. As we move through the pandemic to reach the other side, and as teacher collaboration becomes a more widely accepted norm, it is our hope that educators will take the lessons they learned from their experiences and from those of others and make teacher collaboration a priority for the benefit of their current and future learners.

●●●

References and Further Resources

Fulghum, R. (2003). *All I really need to know I learned in kindergarten: Uncommon thoughts on common things.* Ballantine Penguin Random House.

ABOUT THE AUTHORS

Andrea Honigsfeld, Ed.D, is Professor in the School of Education and Human Services at Molloy College, Rockville Centre, New York. Before entering higher education, she was an English-as-a-foreign-language teacher in Hungary (Grades 5–8 and adult) and an English-as-a-second-language teacher in New York City (Grades K–3 and adult). She also taught Hungarian at New York University. She is the co-author or co-editor of over 25 books and 60 articles and she frequently leads or supports professional learning for educators, primarily focusing on effective differentiated strategies and collaborative practices for multilingual learners.

Maria G. Dove, Ed.D, is Professor in the School of Education and Human Services at Molloy College, Rockville Centre, New York. She teaches about effective instruction for English learners/multilingual learners and guides doctoral students in the Ed.D program in leadership for social justice and equity. Before entering the field of higher education, she worked for over thirty years as an English-as-a-second-language teacher in public school settings (Grades K–12) and in adult English language programs in the greater New York area. Dr. Dove publishes frequently, and along with Dr. Andrea Honigsfeld, she has co-authored multiple best-selling books.

CONTRIBUTORS

Ashley Blackley, co-teacher of multilingual learners and co-founder of Ready-Set-Coteach, is currently a National Board Certified third grade teacher in Raleigh, NC.

Sarah Bouwer, interdisciplinary curriculum specialist and co-founder of Bouwer Braun coaching and consulting, is currently the lead for MS Social Studies for an international school in Shanghai, China.

Allyson Caudill, language specialist and co-founder of Ready-Set-Coteach, is currently a National Board Certified ESL teacher and advocate for multilingual learners in Raleigh, NC.

John Cox, co-teacher of multilingual learners and co-founder of Ready-Set-Coteach, is currently a National Board Certified third grade teacher in Raleigh, NC.

Michelle Gill, a former classroom and ELL teacher, is currently working as a Language Specialist for the Curriculum Department in the Abbotsford School District.

Valentina Gonzalez, a longtime educator and ESL Specialist, is currently an author and educational consultant with Seidlitz Education.

Jackie Griffin, a former language development coach serving culturally and linguistically diverse students, is currently a Director of Curriculum and Professional Development in Skokie, Illinois.

Tan Huynh, a career secondary language specialist in international schools, is also an author, consultant, and podcast host on topics related to language acquisition.

Stephanie Just is a language development coach serving culturally and linguistically diverse students in Buffalo Grove, Illinois.

Lindsay Manzella has been an EAL educator for over 17 years and has taught in Budapest, Hungary; Beirut, Lebanon; and Brooklyn, New York.

Carmen O'Brien is currently in her 8th year of teaching 7th grade ELA in Greenville, Wisconsin.

Kristina Robertson is the Multilingual Program and Equity Administrator for Roseville Public Schools in Minnesota and an author on the Colorin Colorado website. She has 25 years of EL teaching and leadership experience.

Jane Russell Valezy has been an EAL educator for over 20 years, 17 of them in international schools, and currently teaches at the American International School of Budapest, Hungary.

Brittany Schmidt, a former Bilingual/ESL and ELA teacher, is currently a Middle School Associate Principal in Clintonville, Wisconsin.

Katie Toppel, a K-5 language specialist serving multilingual learners through co-teaching, is co-author of the book DIY PD: A Guide to Self-Directed Learning for Educators of Multilingual Learners.

SEIDLITZ EDUCATION

BOOK ORDER FORM

Pricing, specifications, and availability subject to change without notice.

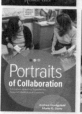

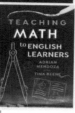

TITLE	PRICE	QTY	TOTAL$
38 Great Academic Language Builders	$24.95		
7 Steps to a Language-Rich Interactive Classroom 2ND ED.	$32.95		
7 Steps To a Language-Rich, Interactive Foreign Language Classroom (LOTE)	$32.95		
Boosting Achievement: Reaching Students with Interrupted or Minimal Education	$26.95		
Content Review & Practice for the TX ESL 154 4TH ED.	$39.95		
Content Review & Practice for the TX Bilingual 164	$39.95		
Content Review & Practice for the TX Spanish 190	$39.95		
Diverse Learner Flip Book 2ND ED.	$29.95		
DIY PD: A Guide to Self-Directed Learning for Teachers of Multilingual Learners NEW!	$29.95		
ELLs in Texas: What Teachers Need to Know 2ND ED.	$34.95		
ELs in Texas: What School Leaders Need to Know 3RD ED.	$34.95		
ELPS Flip Book	$19.95		
English/Spanish Linguistic and Academic Connections	$29.95		
If You Only Knew: Letters from an Immigrant Teacher	$14.99		
Juan José You Are Especial	$9.97		
Mi Cuaderno de Dictado SPANISH	$7.95		
Motivating ELLs: 27 Activities to Inspire & Engage Students	$26.95		
Navigating the ELPS: Using the Standards to Improve Instruction for English Learners	$24.95		
Navigating the ELPS: Math 2ND ED.	$29.95		
Navigating the ELPS: Science	$29.95		
Navigating the ELPS: Social Studies	$29.95		
Navigating the ELPS: Language Arts and Reading	$34.95		
Optimizando el desarrollo de la lectoescritura SPANISH	$39.95		
Pathways to Greatness for ELL Newcomers: A Comprehensive Guide for Schools & Teachers	$32.95		
Portraits of Collaboration	$32.95		
Reading & Writing with English Learners	$29.95		
RTI for ELLs Fold-Out	$16.95		
Sheltered Instruction in Texas: Second Language Acquisition Methods for Teachers of ELs	$29.95		
Small Moves, Big Gains: Teacher Habits that Help Kids To Talk More, Think More, Achieve More	$32.95		
Solved: A Teacher Guide to Making Word Problems Comprehensible	$26.95		
Talk Read Talk Write: A Practical Routine for Learning in All Content Areas K-12 2ND ED.	$32.95		
Teaching Math to English Learners	$24.95		
Teaching Social Studies to ELLs	$24.95		
Teaching Science to English Learners	$24.95		
¡Toma la Palabra! SPANISH	$32.95		
Vocabulary Now! 44 Strategies All Teachers Can Use	$29.95		

HOW TO ORDER

www.seidlitzeducation.com

CALL (210) 315-7119

FAX completed form to (949) 200-4384 with credit card info or attached purchase order

NAME

SHIPPING ADDRESS

CITY   STATE   ZIP

PHONE   EMAIL

Select payment method:

☐ Purchase Order attached
   please make P.O. out to Seidlitz Education

☐ Visa ☐ MasterCard ☐ Discover ☐ AMEX

CARD #

EXPIRES   CVV

SIGNATURE

TAX EXEMPT? please fax a copy of your certificate along with order.

SHIPPING 9% of order total, minimum $14.95
5-7 business days to ship.
If needed sooner please call for rates.

SUBTOTAL	$
DISCOUNT	$
SHIPPING	$
TAX	$
TOTAL	$

REV08/10/22

TITLE	Price	QTY	TOTAL $
Instead Of I Don't Know Poster For the LOTE Classrrom 24" x 36" | **3 pack**			
☐ LOTE FRENCH	$29.85		
☐ LOTE SPANISH	$29.85		
☐ LOTE GERMAN	$29.85		
☐ LOTE ARABIC NEW!	$29.85		
☐ LOTE CHINESE NEW!	$29.85		
		TOTAL $	

TITLE	Price	QTY	TOTAL $
Instead Of I Don't Know Poster, 24" x 36" | **3 pack**			
☐ Elementary ENGLISH	$29.85		
☐ Secondary ENGLISH	$29.85		
Instead Of I Don't Know Posters, 11" x 17"| **20 pack**			
☐ Elementary ENGLISH	$40.00		
☐ Secondary ENGLISH	$40.00		
Instead Of I Don't Know Poster, 24" x 36" | **3 pack** Elementary SPANISH	$29.85		
Instead Of I Don't Know Posters, 11" x 17" | **20 pack** Elementary SPANISH	$40.00		
		TOTAL $	

TITLE	Price	QTY	TOTAL $
Academic Language Cards and Activity Booklet, ENGLISH	$19.95		
Academic Language Cards, SPANISH	$9.95		
		TOTAL $	

Please speak in complete sentences.

TITLE	Price	QTY	TOTAL $
Please Speak In Complete Sentences Poster 24" x 36" | **3 pack** ☐ ENGLISH ☐ SPANISH	$29.85		
Please Speak In Complete Sentences Posters,11" x 17" | **20 pack** ☐ ENGLISH ☐ SPANISH	$40.00		
		TOTAL $	

TAX EXEMPT? please fax a copy of your certificate along with order.	GRAND TOTAL	$
	DISCOUNT	$
SHIPPING 9% of order total, minimum $14.95 5-7 business days to ship. If needed sooner please call for rates.	SHIPPING	$
	TAX	$
	FINAL TOTAL	$

HOW TO ORDER

www.seidlitzeducation.com

CALL (210) 315-7119

FAX completed form to (949) 200-4384 with credit card info or attached purchase order

NAME _____

SHIPPING ADDRESS _____

_____

CITY _____ STATE _____ ZIP _____

PHONE _____ EMAIL _____

Developing language in every classroom.™   **Seidlitz** EDUCATION

Select payment method:

☐ Purchase Order attached
  please make P.O. out to Seidlitz Education

☐ Visa ☐ MasterCard ☐ Discover ☐ AMEX

CARD # _____

EXPIRES _____ CVV _____

SIGNATURE _____